Incidents of Travel in Poetry

Incidents of Travel in Poetry

NEW AND SELECTED POEMS

Frank Lima

EDITED BY GARRETT CAPLES
AND JULIEN POIRIER

City Lights Books | San Francisco

Library of Congress Cataloging-in-Publication Data
Names: Lima, Frank, 1939- | Caples, Garrett T., editor. | Poirier, Julien,
  editor.
Title: Incidents of travel in poetry : new and selected poems / Frank Lima ;
  edited by Garrett Caples, Julien Poirier.
Description: San Francisco : City Lights Books, [2016]
Identifiers: LCCN 2015035462 | ISBN 9780872866676 (softcover)
Subjects: | BISAC: POETRY / American / Hispanic American. | LITERARY
  COLLECTIONS / American / General.
Classification: LCC PS3562.I46 A6 2016 | DDC 811/.54—dc23
LC record available at http://lccn.loc.gov/2015035462

City Lights Books are published at the City Lights Bookstore,
261 Columbus Avenue, San Francisco, CA 94133.
Visit our website: www.citylights.com

Contents

Incidents of Travel in New York: The Lives of Frank Lima

by Garrett Caples

"Frank Lima is a tough man and a gifted poet."
—Kenneth Koch, Untitled Preface to *Inventory: Poems*

A member of the New York School—part of a second-generation group around Frank O'Hara and Kenneth Koch that included David Shapiro, Tony Towle, and Joseph Ceravolo—Frank Lima (1939-2013) is a major Latino poet. Yet throughout his life, Lima rejected both labels (New York School, Latino) in relation to his poetry, and this rejection is one reason why his work remains little known. Indeed, even the massive recent retrospective *New York School Painters & Poets: Neon in Daylight* by Jenni Quilter barely mentions him, though his presence is nonetheless unavoidable: there he is in Alex Katz's painting *The Cocktail Party* (1965), mingling with the likes of Edwin Denby and Rudy Burckhardt; there again in William T. Wood's photograph from the New York City Writers Conference at Wagner College, lurking behind O'Hara and Bill Berkson; and yet again on a Living Theatre handbill, alongside Shapiro, Ceravolo, and others.[1] Though not in the book, Wynn Chamberlain's double portrait of *Poets Dressed and Undressed* (1964) features Lima standing behind the seated trio of O'Hara, Joe Brainard, and Joe LeSueur. That same year, Lima published his first volume, *Inventory: Poems*, with Tibor de Nagy, the gallery that published debuts by O'Hara and Koch, as well as John Ashbery, James Schuyler, and Barbara Guest, and he would also appear in the two New York School anthologies, *The Poets of the*

1. See Jenni Quilter, *New York School Painters & Poets: Neon in Daylight* (Rizzoli, 2014), pages 9, 106, and 131, respectively.

New York School (Pennsylvania, 1969) and *An Anthology of New York Poets* (Random House, 1970). Though he told Guillermo Parra in an interview that he "d[id] not align [his] lifestyle or work with the second generation New York School,"[2] it would be difficult to assemble more evidence of someone being a New York School poet than we can in the case of Frank Lima.

Yet Lima is singular among the New York School, not least because of his ethnicity and class. Where the writers of the New York School tended to be white, highly educated, and middle- to upper-class in origin, Lima was born into poverty in Spanish Harlem on December 27, 1939, the oldest of three sons of a Mexican father, Phillip Lima, and a Puerto Rican mother, Anita Flores Lima. According to Lima's autobiographical poem "Scattered Vignettes," Phillip Lima was the illegitimate son of a doctor, Don Francisco Lima, and a poor Indian woman named Benigna, and was forced to flee Guadalajara after murdering his legitimate half-brother.[3] A prodigious alcoholic, Phillip was a hotel cook, as was Frank's maternal grandfather, and by age 11, Frank was working in kitchens alongside them, laying the foundation for his later professional life as a chef.[4] His mother, also alcoholic, was more educated and is listed as a registered nurse in the entry on Frank in the reference book *Contemporary Authors*.[5] According to "Scattered Vignettes," she also earned money as a *Santera*, or priestess practicing *Santerismo*, an Afro-Caribbean religion syncretizing elements of Roman Catholicism and African spiritual beliefs.[6] The marriage was troubled, and came to an abrupt end when Lima was 12, when the family threw Phillip out of the apartment after he slashed Anita's face with a razor. Homeless and unable to keep a job, Phillip would die of alcoholism in Central Park not long after.[7]

Against this backdrop, the young Frank Lima was subjected to multiple forms of sexual abuse. As an altar boy at St. Cecilia's Roman Catholic Church in East Harlem, he was molested by a priest

2. Guillermo Parra, "NYP: An Interview with Frank Lima," Spring 2001 (posted 7/16/04) (http://interview-franklima.blogspot.com).
3. See "Scattered Vignettes," *Inventory: New & Selected Poems* (Hard Press, 1997), 21-22.
4. Interview with Helen Lima, November 26, 2014.
5. Gale Reference Team, "Biography – Lima, Frank (1939-)" in *Contemporary Authors* (Thomson Gale, 2002).
6. "Scattered Vignettes," *Inventory: New & Selected Poems*, 28-29.
7. *Ibid.*, 29-34.

he refers to in "Scattered Vignettes" as "Father Archangel."[8] In the same poem, he also records the inappropriate behavior of his father, who, drunk, would don Anita's makeup, bra, and nightgown and crawl into his sons' beds "to roughhouse with us."[9] But the greatest trauma stemmed from Anita herself, who, after her husband's death, began having sex with Frank.[10] It would be difficult to overstate how central to both Lima's life and his art this incestuous relationship with his mother is. On the one hand, it sent him into a spiral of self-destruction whose consequences would have lasting effects on his life. On the other hand, this spiral would indirectly lead him into the world of contemporary poetry and the experience of his mother's abuse would form the subject matter of his best-known early poem, "Mom I'm All Screwed Up":

> With popping antennae ringlets
>   you looked like
>   a praying mantis
>   cold cream & turban
>   science fiction gleam
>
>   as real
>   as cancer
>   spreading
>   stuffed-tits-and-rag-guts
>   yawning
>   brillo-crotch
>   that stunk
>   all over me
>   playing
>   Johnny-on-the-pony
>   on me
>   indoors
>
>   The mattress groaned
>   I moaned
>   Mom
>   I'm no horse

8. *Ibid.*, 25-26.
9. *Ibid.*, 24.
10. *Ibid.*, 34.

                you have pimples on your butt
                    your bellybutton droops
                     your boy-pop left
                   the rose of your hopes
                           no
                           no[11]

Such a portrayal of incest seems remote from the stereotypical image of New York School poetry, yet it isn't hard to see why those poets appreciated Lima's work. As Kenneth Koch writes in the untitled preface to *Inventory: Poems*, "In [Lima's] poems there is no moral, and no romantic exaggeration."[12] Later, in the introduction to *Inventory: New & Selected Poems*, David Shapiro would write of Lima's "amazing lack of self-pity,"[13] and the matter-of-fact dissociation from this depiction of his mother's aging body and his own horrible intimacy with it distances Lima's early work from the confessional poetry of the time. Shapiro characterizes this period of Lima's poetry in terms of "the snapshot aesthetic of Robert Frank"[14] and, in their depiction of an impoverished urban landscape, Lima's poems also evoke a certain Beat sensibility; Allen Ginsberg was an early admirer and Lima counted both Ginsberg and Gregory Corso as influences on his work. But, as Shapiro also reports, Lima was critical of the Beat Generation's exaltation of street life: "He said to me, 'You know, I've tried as much as possible to get *away* from the Beat Generation. I tried to get *away* from violence and the old drug habits, and they want to push me back in. . . . Allen always wants to get *back* to Harlem. I want to get *out* of Harlem.'"[15]

Lima's refusal to romanticize his origins seems intimately related to his rejection of ethnic identity in relation to his work. The assumption of identity politics in poetry is that the poet typifies a shared cultural experience to which he or she gives voice. But, as Urayoán Noel writes, "Lima's work mostly eschews the social

11. "Mom I'm All Screwed Up," *Inventory: Poems* (Tibor de Nagy Editions, 1964), 15.
12. Kenneth Koch, Untitled Preface in *Inventory: Poems*, n.p.
13. David Shapiro, "Frank Lima: The Poetry of Everyday Life and the Tradition of American Darkness" in *Inventory: New & Selected Poems*, 17.
14. *Ibid.*, 15.
15. Interview with David Shapiro, December 2, 2014.

voice of the diaspora poet. . . . If there is a political aspect to Lima's work, it has to do with the politics of experience, and with the poet as cataloguer of experiences both transcendent and mundane."[16] Lima's experiences, however, are both too particular and too universal to be crowded under any singular cultural rubric. There is nothing, for example, that marks "Mom I'm All Screwed Up" as Latino, save the inclusion of one word ("mamacita's").[17] His experience of incest, moreover, alienated him from his peers. "When my boyhood friends would boast of / seeing so-and-so's panties," as he writes in "Scattered Vignettes," "I would go home to be with my mother."[18] At the same time, as he told Guillermo Parra in a passionate reflection on his poetics, "the sources [he] dr[e]w on for 'inspiration' are universal":

> I do not want to be a "Latino" poet. That tag is limiting to a particular group and style, although a necessary means as a vehicle and a point to start from, especially for those amongst our people who are not familiar with this peculiar form of writing. . . . But it does not end there, and that is the impression being cast that I do not want to be a part of. I do not feel I have to pontificate to any one of my origins and roots. . . . I do not want to be limited to screaming and bombast for the sake of being heard. That is esthetic colonialism and just too fuck'en [sic] easy to do. Our culture is richer and classier than glorifying El Barrio. . . . We're not just "Latinos." To me, the theater is much bigger than that. It's history and heritage, and a magnificent language that is almost half Arabic. I know this of my own blood, half Mexican and half Puerto Rican that I am. This is my culture, not one or the other.[19]

Lima's disinclination to be labeled a "Latino" poet is thus a nuanced one. He deconstructs the category by pointing out he's from "two Latino cultures,"[20] as if to suggest "Latino" isn't particular enough, while he broadens the parameters of what it means to come from a Spanish-speaking culture by invoking

16. Urayoán Noel, *In Visible Movement: Nuyorican Poetry from the Sixties to Slam* (University of Iowa Press, 2014), 6.
17. "Mom I'm All Screwed Up," *Inventory: Poems*, 16.
18. "Scattered Vignettes," *Inventory: New & Selected Poems*, 35.
19. Guillermo Parra, "NYP: An Interview with Frank Lima."
20. *Ibid.*

the Arabic influence on the formation of the language, through the Moorish conquest of the Iberian peninsula. His rejection of "glorifying El Barrio" perhaps harkens back to advice he received from Frank O'Hara: "you can't write about prison and drugs all your life or you won't last that long."[21] Despite his initial success as a poet of street life, Lima knew he couldn't maintain such subject matter because he wanted both to survive and to pursue more diverse themes. One senses too, in the disavowal of "screaming and bombast," the estrangement Lima felt in particular from the performance-oriented writers of the Nuyorican Poets Café who emerged in the 1970s. Julio Marzán, a Puerto Rican poet from Harlem who became close friends with Lima in the 1980s, describes the perspective he and Frank shared on the Nuyorican Movement:

> [Nuyorican Poets Café co-founder] Miguel Algarín taught poetry but he really wasn't a critic. He tried to justify it as, these are not poems, look at them as voices. They always tried to get away from any literary criticism. It's with that kind of thing that they would shove aside anybody with any serious artistic or literary pretentions—they always found some justification for being authentic, that would be the rationale behind the poetry. . . . Any organization that encouraged you to read somebody because of where they came from was overreaching and not focusing on whether the poetry was any good or not.[22]

To be sure, Lima felt ambivalence, even bitterness, in this stance; in the same interview with Parra, he speaks of the "terribly high" price he paid in his exclusion "from New York P[uerto]R[ican] anthologies and other events celebrating our culture."[23] But as Parra suggests in an email, it may be that Lima "was simply way ahead of his time,"[24] given Pedro López Adorno's contention that Lima is "an important precursor" to "younger Nuyorican poets . . . the major framework of [whose] poetic endeavor centers on

21. Bob Holman, "The Resurrection of Frank Lima: An Investigative Poem," *Poets & Writers* (September-October, 2000), 35.
22. Interview with Julio Marzán, Feburary 19, 2015.
23. Guillermo Parra, "NYP: An Interview with Frank Lima."
24. Guillermo Parra, Email, January 25, 2015.

25. Pedro López Adorno, "Making the Decolonized Visible: Puerto Rican Poetry of the Last Four Decades," *Centro Journal*, Vol. XVIII(2) fall 2006, 15.
26. Bob Holman, "The Resurrection of Frank Lima," 33, 39.
27. "Scattered Vignettes," *Inventory: New & Selected Poems*, 35.
28. Even here, Lima introduces biographical uncertainty, for, in the Holman interview, he claims this stint occurred on nearby Hart Island, though most evidence—including Sherman Drexler's account (see http://www.brooklynrail.org/2009/07/art/sherman-drexler-with-phong-bui) and Lima's remarks elsewhere—points to North Brother Island. Paul Pines suggests Lima was in a detox program on Hart Island in the late '60s, so Frank is perhaps accidentally conflating the two in his interview with Holman. Yet, given that the Holman interview is presented as an "investigative poem," with line breaks and so forth, I can't help wondering whether Lima is deliberately condensing and poeticizing his experience, insofar as Hart Island also contains New York City's potter's field, where his father

the individual and his/her search for a liberating identity articulated from the social, historical, political, and economic displacements the respective subjects have had to endure."[25]

★

"Frank Lima is an American Villon."
—David Shapiro, Interview, 12/2/14

There's an almost mythic quality to Frank Lima's life, in that it is rife with striking detail, but its particulars are hard to nail down. Indeed, he seems to deliberately muddy the waters. In his interview with Bob Holman for *Poets & Writers*, for example, Lima claims he started using heroin at age 12, was an addict for 25 years, and finally kicked the habit in 1972.[26] But he was 12 in 1951, so the math doesn't quite work out. This is simply to say that our account is necessarily provisional, pending a full-scale biography. What is clear, however, is that, following the repeated sexual violations by his mother, Lima became a gang member, leading to his first encounters with the criminal justice system. "My first arrest took place in junior high school: / a gun," he writes in "Scattered Vignettes." "My second arrest: a gun, etc. / I was in a club called / The Young Demons. / We were into guns, / drugs and territory."[27] At age 14, he dropped out of school altogether and, by 1956, when Lima was 17, his gun arrests and heroin addiction conspired to land him in a juvenile drug rehabilitation program at Riverside Hospital on North Brother Island in the East River.[28] Lima would be in and out of this program every six months until 1960, when he aged out of it. And though it failed to keep him off heroin, the program nonetheless proved to be Lima's salvation, in the form of his encounter with the painter Sherman Drexler. Drexler was teaching art at North Brother Island when he "first met the young poet Frank Lima who begged me to allow him not to paint in my class." According to Drexler, Lima "was influenced by Keats and Shelley and had not yet found his real voice. I lent him books by Tristan Corbière, François Villon, and William Carlos Williams."[29] That Drexler perceived Lima to already have poetic influences contrasts somewhat with Lima's own recollection, which implies that he only began writing after their encounter:

> One day he came in with *Life Studies* / by Robert Lowell, when it first came out. / I was amazed—I thought, I'd like to write / like that, and I told Sherman. He said, / Why don't you write then? / I was flabbergasted that he'd ask / such a question. I told him quite frankly / I didn't know anything about writing, / in fact, and I remember telling him this / exactly, I don't even know the English / language. Sherman looked at me, // I'll never forget it, and said, "Well, you can talk, / can't you? Why don't you write like you talk?" // And it hit me, I could see the words / we said, the colorful, the real language / . . . of the street, I could all of a sudden see / it written down and staying real. // It was like a code, but when I wrote it down, / because I did, that's when I began to write, / it was like it became something else.[30]

Whether or not Lima had written poetry prior to meeting Drexler is ultimately immaterial, for their encounter obviously galvanized the young poet; Drexler's epiphanic advice to "write like you talk" led to Lima's earliest mature work, which the painter promptly shared with his poet friends, including Lowell himself, as well as Koch and O'Hara.[31] These poets responded with enthusiasm and sent Lima their books, and among the other poets he recalled reading at this time are Ginsberg, Corso, Apollinaire, and Baudelaire.[32]

But although during his stay on North Brother Island, Lima would also meet Elaine de Kooning,[33] with whom he became close and who later painted his portrait, there's a roughly two-year gap between his final discharge from the program in 1960 and his meet-

was buried, as was Puerto Rican poet Julia de Burgos (1914-1953), before she was disinterred and brought back to Puerto Rico. In the Holman interview, Lima claims that, the last time he saw his father, his father was with de Burgos, sharing a bottle in Central Park. But this is almost certainly a poetic invention, based on de Burgos's similar and contemporaneous alcoholic collapse and death, and intimate friends like David Shapiro and Tony Towle suggest Lima was not above such embellishments. For Lima's discussion of Hart Island, see Bob Holman, "The Resurrection of Frank Lima," 30-32, 43. For Paul Pines's discussion of Lima, see "Jon Curley with Paul Pines," http://theconversant.org/?p=7201.

29. See "In Conversation: Sherman Drexler with Phong Bui," *Brooklyn Rail*, July-August 2009, http://www.brooklynrail.org/2009/07/art/sherman-drexler-with-phong-bui.

30. Bob Holman, "The Resurrection of Frank Lima," 31. While I have noted Holman's line and stanza breaks, I haven't attempted to reproduce his layout here.

31. See Bob Holman, "The Resurrection of Frank Lima," 31-32 and "In Con-

ing with O'Hara, Koch, and other poets of the New York School in 1962. According to Tim Keane, at this time Lima was living with Keane's uncle, the painter Bob Corless, in a loft at 47 East Broadway.[34] This period probably accounts for the development of two of Frank's major non-poetry preoccupations. The first of these was boxing. The evidence is scant and anecdotal, though it seems he boxed in the New York Golden Gloves tournament. Ron Padgett recalls "ask[ing] Frank about his life as a boxer":

> He gave me a short history of how he had started, in East Harlem, through the Police Athletic League, who were getting tough kids off the street and into constructive activities (like hitting each other!). He'd taken up boxing and he was pretty good at it. . . . Frank said it was either in that Golden Gloves match, or one around that time, when he stepped into the ring . . . he looked into the eyes of his opponent and it suddenly struck him that this man facing him didn't want to defeat him, this man wanted to *kill* him. The look of ferocity in the guy's eyes was horrendous, and in fact the guy turned out to be unbelievably ferocious and vicious. Frank said that afterward he said to himself: "I don't want to be competing with people who are trying to actually kill me." Around the same time a boxer named Benny "The Kid" Paret was killed in the ring. That was probably on Frank's mind.[35]

Though little is known about Lima's boxing career, it certainly contributed to his Villonesque mystique among the members of the New York School, who witnessed the occasional flash of his prowess. (Once, according to Tony Towle, at a party at de Kooning's, Lima was teased into a demonstration by one of Joe Louis's sparring partners, George "Baby Dutch" Culbertson, whom he promptly knocked over a table.)[36] That he was affected by Afro-Cuban boxer Benny "The Kid" Paret's death in the ring in April 1962 is evident from a poem on the subject that appears in *Inventory: Poems*.[37] But while Lima had already hung up his gloves

versation: Sherman Drexler with Phong Bui."
32. Bob Holman, "The Resurrection of Frank Lima," 32
33. *Ibid.*
34. Email from Tim Keane, April 23, 2015.
35. Interview with Ron Padgett, January 13, 2015.
36. Interview with Tony Towle, January 7, 2015; I owe the name of this sparring partner to Tim Keane, "Recurring Waves of Arrival: Elaine de Kooning's Portraits from Loft Dwellers to JFK" (http://hyperallergic.com/197744/recurring-waves-of-arrival-elaine-de-koonings-portraits-from-loft-dwellers-to-jfk/).
37. "The Memory of Benny (Kid) Paret," *Inventory: Poems*, 13–14.

by the time he entered the New York School milieu, he maintained a lifelong interest in the sport, even hosting "fight night" dinners for various poets during major pay-per-view matches in the early 2000s.[38]

The other preoccupation from these years is his professional development as a chef. Again, not much information is available concerning his formal training. The article on Lima in *Contemporary Authors* lists him as the recipient of the New York Hotel Exposition French Classical Cookery Award in 1959,[39] suggesting his training overlapped with his stays on North Brother Island. According to Seth Rogovoy, who interviewed him in 1996 for the *Berkshire Eagle*, Lima "was cooking in top New York restaurants in his early 20s, including the Essex House and with the late Pierre Franey."[40] But Lima served his primary apprenticeship under René Verdon, who went on to fame as the first executive chef of the White House, during the Kennedy administration.[41] Lima even claimed to have helped Verdon prepare at least one meal for the Kennedy White House, though little is known about this beyond the bare fact,[42] and Frank ultimately didn't join his mentor down in D.C. By all accounts, Lima was an extraordinary chef, though, while proud of his ability, he apparently derived little pleasure from cooking, associating it perhaps with his abusive father. In any case, he wouldn't commit to cooking as a full-time profession until the late '70s.

But the signal event of Lima's life in the early '60s was meeting, not JFK, but rather Frank O'Hara and Kenneth Koch at the New York City Writers Conference at Wagner College, on Staten Island, in August 1962. There Lima would also meet two of his lifelong friends, Joe Ceravolo and the still-teenaged David Shapiro. Not only was Lima given a scholarship to attend, but he and Shapiro were the co-recipients of the Gotham Book Mart Avant-Garde Poetry Award. "Kenneth [Koch] gave the prize to me and

38. See Bob Holman, "The Resurrection of Frank Lima," 41; Shapiro, Towle, Marzán, Holman, and Anselm Berrigan all confirm attending these gatherings. Some of these parties were co-hosted by another poet friend of Lima's, Vicki Hudspith.
39. Gale Reference Team, "Biography – Lima, Frank (1939-)."
40. Seth Rogovoy, "Frank Lima: Poet Back from the Edge," *Berkshire Eagle* (October 31, 1996), archived at http://www.berkshireweb.com/rogovoy/thebeat/beat1031.html.
41. According to Lima, "I will always be René Verdon's apprentice in cooking, and / Frank O'Hara's in poetry." Bob Holman, "The Resurrection of Frank Lima," 39.
42. Interview with Helen Lima, November 26, 2014.

43. Interview with David Shapiro, December 2, 2014. According to Tony Towle, the prize amounted to $100 (Email from Tony Towle, May 15, 2015).

44. Gale Reference Team, "Biography – Lima, Frank (1939-)."

45. Interview with David Shapiro, December 2, 2014. Though Lima's poem appears in a section of the anthology of poetry by fellow travelers, i.e., sympathetic non-African Americans, Shapiro suggests that Hughes was also making a point about the African heritage of Puerto Rico, further complicating Lima's sense of what it meant to be Latino.

46. In "The Resurrection of Frank Lima," 34, Lima claims he took O'Hara's 1963 workshop at the New School, a circumstance also recorded in Brad Gooch's *City Poet: The Life and Times of Frank O'Hara* (Knopf, 1993), 400, but Tony Towle, who took O'Hara's workshop, insists this isn't true (Email from Tony Towle, May 18, 2015).

47. Bob Holman, "The Resurrection of Frank Lima," 33.

to Frank Lima," Shapiro says, "and now I can say that secretly he said, 'You know, David, you don't really need this money, your father's a doctor, but would you mind if I gave the prize money to Frank?' I said, 'No, that's wonderful.' He gave the prize to Frank and I know that Frank used it well."[43] This detail seems characteristic of the regard in which Lima was held by his fellow poets, who did what they could to direct money to the impoverished young writer; he would also receive grants from the Academy of American Poets in 1962 and the John Hay Whitney Foundation in 1965,[44] this latter at the behest of Robert Lowell and Langston Hughes, who included Lima's poem on Benny Paret in the anthology *The Poetry of the Negro, 1746-1970* (Doubleday, 1970).[45] His new friends would also help Lima land his first publication, in the *Evergreen Review*, which printed "Pudgy" and "Hotel Park (East 110th Street)" in issue 27 in 1962.

While both Koch and O'Hara became mentors to Lima at this time, it was O'Hara in particular who took Frank under his wing.[46] Unlike Koch, who imposed a professorial distance, O'Hara offered drinking and companionship, bringing Lima everywhere from the symphony to the Cedar Tavern. Through O'Hara, Frank would meet the likes of poet/ballet critic Edwin Denby, composer Virgil Thomson, and choreographer George Balanchine. "I had no idea who these people were," Lima told Bob Holman, "except that they were open, and different, and funny, and they had a sense of life that inspired me, and they accepted me. I was born and raised in Spanish Harlem, in the Barrio, here I was in the middle of the avant-garde art world. Unbelievable."[47] This musical exposure would have lasting effect, as Lima became a devotee of classical music for the rest of his life. O'Hara also took an interest in Lima's personal well-being, allowing him, during a period of relapse and homelessness, to sleep on the couch at the East Ninth Street apartment the older poet shared with Joe LeSueur. O'Hara went as far as organizing an art sale through Tibor de Nagy to raise money for Lima to see a psychotherapist.[48] The two Franks also collaborated on a play, *Love on the Hoof* (1963), intended for an unrealized Andy Warhol film project called *Messy Lives*. Joe LeSueur even recalled coming home one evening during this period to find a drunk O'Hara and Lima "buck naked, fooling around with each other."[49]

Such an encounter between the two poets was seemingly an isolated event, while LeSueur's astonished reaction—blurting out the question, "What are you two doing?"—had less to do with his experience of O'Hara's promiscuity than with his perception of Lima's heterosexuality. With his handsome, brooding looks and streetwise charm, Lima was something of a ladies man, though prone to infidelity and still dogged by his drug problem. The period during which he slept on O'Hara's couch probably coincided with the end of Lima's first marriage. David Shapiro and Tony Towle both suggest Lima's first wife was a black woman, the titular character of the poem "Pudgy" whom Frank apostrophizes as "o my chocolate princess."[50] Their relationship is depicted as passionate but violent, and interrupted by periods of incarceration. "He was done with that [marriage] by the time I met him," recalls Towle, who, by June 1963, would find himself sharing the same East Ninth Street apartment with Lima after it was vacated by O'Hara and LeSueur. While roommates, Lima and Towle would see little of each other as both were pursuing love affairs elsewhere, though they became close after Frank moved out that September to move into an apartment on Second Avenue with Sheyla Baykal, an artist's model working with Elaine de Kooning.[51] "They made quite a glamorous couple without even trying," Ron Padgett recalls, and Baykal and Lima would soon marry. She not only is depicted alongside Frank in Katz's *Cocktail Party* but also is the dedicatee of the final two poems in his first collection, *Inventory: Poems*.

48. Brad Gooch, *City Poet*, 401.
49. Joe LeSueur, *Digressions on Some Poems by Frank O'Hara* (FSG, 2003), 292.
50. Interview with David Shapiro, December 2, 2014; Interview with Tony Towle, January 7, 2015; *Inventory: Poems*, 19.
51. Interview with Tony Towle, January 7, 2015.

Like many people, Lima was deeply affected by the 1966 death of Frank O'Hara. Because O'Hara personally constituted a social nexus for so many artists and writers, his death, in some sense, brought a premature end to a major phase of the New York School. "Those 60 or more people that Larry [Rivers] said considered [O'Hara] their best friend, in New York alone, after Frank died, the cohesion dissipated and I simply did not see much of any of those people," Bill Berkson recalls.[52] That same year marked the founding of the Poetry Project at St. Mark's Church in-the-Bowery in the East Village, and there was a certain divide between those New York School poets—like Padgett, Berkson, Jim Brodey, Ted Berrigan—who aligned themselves with the late '60s counterculture and those—like Lima, Towle, and Ceravolo—who did not. Some of Lima's distance from the scene also resulted from his continuing struggle with heroin. When, for example, Padgett and Shapiro began preparing the *New York Poets* anthology in 1967, Lima was the only contributor unable to supply an author photo, because he was in jail at the time.[53] Still later, in 1968, Towle recalls running into Lima in Washington Square Park:

> He seemed a little funny but I didn't think too much of it. We were supposed to read together at St. Mark's Church; it was my first reading there, in October '68. This was probably Frank's first reading there as well. He was late and Anne Waldman was saying, "Oh, where's Frank?" And then all of a sudden, it hit me: when I ran into him at the park, Frank was high. Not drunk but high. So I told Anne, "I don't think he's coming, I think we ought to start." So I did the whole reading; I read both parts because he never showed up.[54]

52. Interview with Bill Berkson, January 28, 2015.
53. Interview with Ron Padgett, January 13, 2015; Interview with David Shapiro, December 2, 2014.
54. Interview with Tony Towle, January 7, 2015.

Not long after this episode, Lima checked himself into a rehabilitation program on Hart Island in the East River. A typed letter to Paul Pines—a poet living in the same Second Avenue building as Lima—is dated December 29, 1968, and announces Frank's intention to remain there "for some time." This stay on Hart Island was a pivotal time in Lima's life, even if he continued to struggle with addiction until '72. Accompanying the letter was a MS of poems, already titled *Underground with the Oriole*, which Lima asked Pines to Xerox four times and give to Towle to edit, with an eye toward submitting it to Columbia University Press for the 1969 Frank O'Hara Award for Poetry. Though it didn't win, an expanded version of *Underground* was accepted by E.P. Dutton and published in 1971, as Lima's first full-length and first generally available book. This period between his time at Hart and the publication of *Underground* coincides with the end of his marriage to Sheyla and the beginning of his third marriage, to a woman named Sara. According to *Contemporary Authors*, Lima had two daughters with Sara, Natasha and Nanushka, though apparently neither was his biological offspring.[55]

This period also marks Lima's transition into work as a drug counselor and nonprofit executive, beginning at Phoenix House Foundation, an organization established around the concept of ex-addicts counseling other recovering addicts that originally based itself on Hart. By 1975, he would be the executive director of Compass House, whose program specifically catered to teenage drug abusers. This is listed as his occupation in the author note of his second full-length collection, *Angel (New Poems)*, published by Liveright in 1976.[56] In the interim between *Underground* and *Angel*, Frank divorced Sara and remarried yet again, to Roberta Brancifiorti, in 1974. He also earned an M.F.A., despite his lack of even a high school diploma, from Columbia University, in 1975; that he was able to enroll was undoubtedly due to the influence of Kenneth Koch, who, along with Stanley Kunitz, served as Lima's primary advisor.

But even as he received this academic validation and published his second book, Lima began to withdraw from the poetry scene.

55. See "The Author" note in *Underground with the Oriole* (Dutton, 1971), 93; Gale Reference Team, "Biography – Lima, Frank (1939–)"; Email from Helen Lima, April 9, 2015.
56. See the author note on the back cover of *Angel (New Poems)* (Liveright, 1976); Gale Reference Team, "Biography – Lima, Frank (1939–)."

The reasons for this were several. In 1976, his son Matthew was born, followed by his daughter Christophe in 1983, and the financial pressures of starting a family no doubt accounted for Lima's return to the work of professional cookery. He began a series of demanding, high-end executive chef positions, including at the World Trade Center restaurant, Windows on the World, and at the corporate cafeteria at Citibank, before finally in the late '80s becoming an instructor at the New York Restaurant School (now the Art Institute of New York), until his retirement in 2007.[57] Teaching cooking, it seems, was more fulfilling for Lima than cooking itself. At the same time, having finally kicked heroin, Lima had become an alcoholic. Late into his tenure directing Compass House, "he had got to the point where he got there in the morning and opened his drawer, and took a slug out of a bottle that he had there," according to Tony Towle.[58] The physical damage of a lifetime of substance abuse came to a head with a diagnosis of cirrhosis of the liver, but Lima managed to arrest the progress of the disease by quitting drinking, with the help of a detox program at Roosevelt Hospital.[59] Achieving complete sobriety for the first time in his adult life drove Lima further away from the poetry world; not only did he need to avoid the hard-drinking atmosphere of places like the Cedar Tavern, but, as he seems to imply in his interview with Bob Holman, he had difficulty writing poems in the absence of drugs and alcohol.[60] As the 1980s began, Lima's life as a poet had seemingly ended.

★

57. Interview with Helen Lima, November 26, 2014.
58. Interview with Tony Towle, January 7, 2015.
59. Bob Holman, "The Resurrection of Frank Lima," 39.
60. Ibid., 40.

"It's not that I feel like I'm back. I feel like // I'm here for the first time"
—Frank Lima in "The Resurrection of Frank Lima"

Had Lima never resumed writing, he might rate as an extraordinary but minor poet, one of several colorful footnotes of New York School poetry. But his silence was not to last. "In the late

'80s," he told Bob Holman, "I was clean, / unhappily married, and desperate. / I started to write again as the marriage / ended."[61] While Lima's earlier poems increasingly incorporated a surrealist tendency toward irrational imagery, as far back as the second half of *Underground*, the later work might be seen as the full realization of this impulse:

> I found the words in a box and became recklessly enamored with
> Them. As I watched, they blew smoke rings into my sacramental
> Face. I was a blind old man, unzipping my life before them and
> Trembling at the touch of cold marble. My fingers were once wild
>
> Pigeons perched on the statues and I would sacrifice my soul for the
> Erotic stillness of yesterday. The words would arrive through the nail
> Holes in the century wearing the flickering faces of the past. I fit myself
> Into anyone that will have me, who will shoot at me with the hours of a
>
> Wheelchair. When will I stop looking over my shoulder in the subway?
> I collected the tickets at the door, and made it perfectly clear that
> Writing is as lonely as a pile of discarded shoes. Heaven is wingless and
> Far away and there are no books that mention your name or mine.

This poem, "01.03.2000," is typical of Lima's later style. Frequently untethered to any recognizable, realistic scenario, even as they often seem to deliberate on the act of writing itself, the poems move matter-of-factly, almost effortlessly, from assertion to assertion, with no obvious sense of logical development. Yet they seem the opposite of random phrasemaking, instead motivated by an inner emotional necessity. Intriguingly, in light of his more open-field-like compositions of the '60s, the format of evenly divided quatrains—sometimes varied as tercets or quintains—predominates. Filip Marinovich, a poet who attended Lima's workshops at the Poetry Project around 2000, offers insight into Lima's compositional process:

61. *Ibid.*

It's not like he would write quatrains. He would just free-write. He even had these Xeroxes of Peter Elbow's freewriting manual from the '70s or '80s, whenever that came out. And he would just freewrite and divide it up into quatrains. . . . And there was something about that new form that allowed him to write poetry where he felt like he couldn't write poetry before because it was part of the whole vortex of addictions. So he found a new form for it and he was very defensive about that and very proud that he had found a new form after all this struggle.[62]

This comment is revealing insofar as it supports those characterizations of Lima's later work as surrealist.[63] Any distinction here between freewriting and automatic writing is probably academic, and it seems clear that the use of Peter Elbow's techniques resulted in a form of automatism that liberated Lima's imagination in the absence of mind-altering substances. In his interview with Guillermo Parra, it's easy to hear the criticisms Lima makes of Ginsberg ("the literary [death] that Allen suffered") and Jean-Michel Basquiat ("he was naive and lacked what it takes to live without getting loaded") as a negative articulation of the defensive pride about his own reinvention as a poet that Marinovich refers to above.[64]

Lima's discovery of freewriting techniques revitalized his practice as a poet. Yet he remained aloof from the poetry world, due to his work and family life. His marriage to Roberta effectively ended by 1988, when he would move out of their apartment in Flushing, Queens, though he remained nearby to help raise their children. At the beginning of 1989, however, Lima met Helen Hansen, a CPA who was the sister of a student in his class at the New York Restaurant School. Helen would move in with Lima several months after they started seeing each other, though they wouldn't marry until 1992, due to his lingering divorce proceedings.[65] After four previous failed marriages, Lima would remain

62. Interview with Filip Marinovich, February 3, 2015.
63. See, for example, David Shapiro, "Frank Lima: The Poetry of Everyday Life" in *Inventory: New & Selected Poems*, and Garrett Caples, "Surrealism Is a Romantic Critique of the Avant-Garde from Within," http://www.poetryfoundation.org/harriet/2014/11/surrealism-is-a-romantic-critique-of-the-avant-garde-from-within/?woo.
64. Guillermo Parra, "NYP: An Interview with Frank Lima."
65. Interview with Helen Lima, November 26, 2014.

with Helen for the rest of his life. And soon he'd be drawn back to the poetry world. In 1997, Hard Press, a small Massachusetts publisher, brought out Lima's *Inventory: New & Selected Poems*, edited with an introduction by David Shapiro. The driving force behind this volume was the poet Michael Gizzi and while the edition was small—probably 500 copies—it served to put Lima back on the poetry map; over the course of the next few years, Lima would find himself featured in such places as the *American Poetry Review* and the Poetry Society of America, and even on the cover of *Poets & Writers*.[66] He also taught workshops at the Poetry Project and in Riverdale, and gave a number of readings.

Much of this activity was preparatory to a new collection Lima had written, *The Beatitudes*, an incendiary volume of invectives against the Judeo-Christian tradition, inspired by his reading of Anne Sexton's work and his own experiences of abuse in the Catholic Church.[67] The book was announced, was scheduled for publication in 2000, and even went as far as being typeset, but ultimately never appeared. The reasons aren't entirely clear but the present publisher of Hard Press, Anne Bei, believes the cancellation stemmed from the bursting of the dot.com bubble, during which the press was in the midst of an abortive restructuring into an online venture called Cultureport. When Hard Press re-emerged, its focus had shifted exclusively to art and art criticism.[68] But by then, *The Beatitudes* had already been accepted by another small press, Black Square Editions, which proceeded to string Lima along with promises to publish it for several years before he finally withdrew the MS.[69] The failure of *Beatitudes* to appear was a source of great bitterness to Lima, destroying the momentum of his comeback in the poetry world. This, combined with an unsuccessful attempt to stage a libretto he wrote about the king and queen of Mexico, led him to abandon further attempts at publication, though he remained willing to contribute poems and give readings when asked.

66. Lima appeared in the July-August 2000 issue of *APR*, was interviewed by the Poetry Society (http://www.poetrysociety.org/psa/poetry/crossroads/qa_american_poetry/frank_lima/), and was interviewed by Bob Holman for the September-October 2000 issue of *Poets & Writers*.
67. Bob Holman, "The Resurrection of Frank Lima," 41-42.
68. Email from Anne Bei, April 21, 2015.
69. Phone conversation with Frank Lima, circa 2012; Interview with Helen Lima, November 26, 2014.

Yet despite this disappointment, the last two decades of Lima's life were probably his happiest. "Hearing him read from *Inventory* in the late '90s was an intense experience," Anselm Berrigan writes. "The man went through so much as a kid and young man, and seemed to be at a real high point in the years I most interacted with him—roughly '97 through '03/'04, maybe. A renaissance of sorts—his love of poetry was very pure, and he clearly leaned on it for survival purposes."[70] According to Helen, his kids were his top priority, so she and Frank would live together in Flushing—punctuated by frequent vacations to Cancún, which Frank fell in love with on their honeymoon—until 2004, after his daughter Christophe graduated from college. They then bought a house on Lido Beach, Long Island. "Frank loved the beach," Helen recalls. "He always felt happy with the fact that he started out in Spanish Harlem and then he ended up here in Lido Beach, which is not such a poor neighborhood."[71] Perhaps most importantly, regardless of the state of his poetry "career"—and the move to Long Island served to further isolate him from the poetry scene as such—Lima only grew more prolific in the last decade of his life, owing to an encounter with Kenneth Koch before the latter's 2002 death from leukemia. As Helen recalls:

> The subway ride was like 45 minutes for him to go to work. . . . He used to write every single day on the train ride. And when Kenneth Koch had passed, Frank had gone to visit him in the hospital . . . . Kenneth told Frank that you have to write every single day. When you write, it's not like someone doing a job. This has to come from you. . . . Frank tried really, really hard to write a poem every day.[72]

As a result, there are hundreds—more likely thousands—of pages of poetry from the last decade of his life. Even allowing for his inevitable culling of inferior pieces and perhaps an occasional day off, he would have composed in excess of 3,500 poems. Given

70. Email from Anselm Berrigan, January 31, 2015.
71. Interview with Helen Lima, November 26, 2014.
72. *Ibid.*

the small number of previous collections—the two versions of *Inventory, Underground,* and *Angel*—it's safe to say the bulk of Lima's poetry remains unpublished. But it is with this late work that we can ultimately support the claim that Lima is a major poet. For here Lima developed a distinctive mode that accommodated everything from the quotidian to the literary and historical to the most exalted displays of surrealist imagination. This is why, in the present publication, even as we include a significant selection of earlier work, we emphasize Lima's uncollected and/or unpublished poems. The world has yet to experience the extent of his poetic genius.

In the early '60s, on the advice of Frank O'Hara, Lima had developed the habit of dating his poems in order to keep track of his periods of inspiration,[73] but this practice takes on an obsessive intensity in the MSS of later work, as though to maintain the discipline of his vow of daily composition. Among this later work, it's not uncommon to find an elaborate poem of several pages bearing a single day's date. His productivity was augmented by a tendency to write responses to poems by his friends, particularly David Shapiro and Vicki Hudspith. Only in the last year of his life, which was beset with health problems, did his output diminish. Bad advice from a physician convinced him he would be able to tolerate alcohol in strict moderation, but this was not the case. Late in 2012, he began to experience a loss of appetite coupled with water retention; only after months of misdiagnosis did doctors realize that his liver was failing. Helen brought him to Mt. Sinai Hospital and he was put on the list for a transplant. But by Spring 2013, he'd seemingly made a miraculous full recovery, "walking around Manhattan . . . like nothing happened," his wife says.[74] The diagnosis was so good, the couple wanted to make another trip to Cancún, though his doctors advised them to wait a few months to be sure he'd regained his health. Then in June, Lima began to decline again, victim of a stroke that eluded

73. Bob Holman, "The Resurrection of Frank Lima," 41–42.
74. Interview with Helen Lima, November 26, 2014.

diagnosis until September. All of his organs began to fail. He died on Monday, October 21, 2013. "He struggled so hard; he wanted to get better," Helen Lima says. "The day he passed away, that Sunday, he woke up in the morning and it came right off his lips. 'Helen, when are we gonna go to Cancún again? I still want to take you to Cancún.'"[75] It's an expression of both romantic longing and the will to live characteristic of a poet for whom poetry represented an escape from suffering and, as Berrigan suggests, a means of survival.

San Francisco, 2015

75. *Ibid.*

A Note on the Text
by Julien Poirier

Frank Lima published almost nothing after 1997—though, if asked, he wouldn't hesitate to send new work to completely unknown poetry journals in New York City. I remember passing around fresh Lima manuscripts at Ugly Duckling Presse in 2002, just months before the entire run of our magazine featuring those poems went up in a house fire. By then I was already a Lima fan, having torn through 1997's *Inventory* during the dog days in Manhattan. Still, as great as it was, nothing in that book prepared me for the new poems I saw in the early aughts: These were Prospero-level spells that outstripped even the iconoclastic hit jobs I'd read, courtesy of Filip Marinovich, in Lima's unpublished and possibly cursed *Beatitudes*—messages in a bottle sent from a darkly enchanted island that I had to somehow reach.

The only problem was that no one seemed to have the keys to that shore. Frank himself wanted to publish *Beatitudes* first, and early discussions with Garrett Caples focused on that book, or possibly an updated Selected. Indeed, none of the poems that appear in the second half of the present volume were available to us until just after the poet's death, when Frank's widow generously shipped the whole trove to Garrett. At which point, we were strongly inclined to publish (and to read) nothing else.

And we may have even done that—but then, what about Lima's earlier books, all of them out of print? So few contemporary readers, even other poets, were really familiar with them—and they were so good. We would need to include a selection from those books in ours—a very generous one, narrower than Shapiro's in *Inventory* but as vital in its own way. So taking Shapiro's Lima as the touchstone of 20th-Century Frank, playing with and against that selection of new (in 1997) and older poems, we assembled ours. Consider it a scenic ride on the Lima local, occasionally running express as it approaches the island city of the poet's most fully integrated work.

Of course, any superlative is slippery when it comes to Lima's poetry. Is the new stuff really *better* than the amazing coming-out-of-nowhere early poems? Considering the force of those poems, and the across-the-board fineness of work from every phase of his career, we were looking to get a good core sample for this book. And so we tried to keep the contours of all the phases: To show the Ponge-flecked lines bridging *Angel* and the Neruda nudes of *Tulum* dissolving into the daily bread and subway winds of *Orfeo*.

A little more about that process of selection: quite late in the game we noticed that Frank had edited several of his earlier published poems upon republishing them in 1997. These edits ranged from tweaks (a dropped hyphen or comma) to torques (a line dropped or switched in order; even, to one poem, a few new lines added). And then, too, we found small differences when poems appearing in the original *Inventory*, a chapbook, reappeared in *Underground with the Oriole*. The question was whether or not to record these changes in *Incidents*; and with all due respect to Frank, we elected to publish the poems as they originally appeared in his two full-length books, *Oriole* and *Angel*, therefore favoring *Oriole*'s versions to the first *Inventory*'s but overriding all small changes to those same poems and others that Frank made at a roughly 30-year remove in the late '90s.

While *Incidents of Travel in Poetry* showcases the better part of an eponymous manuscript sent by Helen Lima to Garrett Caples in 2014, the kicker is that our selection is little more than a taste of late Lima. Frank may have stopped ordering his poems into manuscripts in 2006, but he was still writing them all the time; and, already overtaxed by the embarrassment of riches in *Incidents*, we haven't included *a single poem* from that later period—a full seven years of uncharted terrain. We've also depicted the florid *retablos* of *Beatitudes* (a full book in the wings) in silhouette here. Space constraints, yes—and plenty of whole cloth for future editors, whom we can only envy.

Acknowledgments

This book is dedicated to David Shapiro and Christophe and Matt Lima. The editors would also like to dedicate their work to Helen Lima.

The editors would like to thank the following people for lending their assistance and/or helping make this book possible:

Nico Alvarado, Anne Bei, Bill Berkson, Anselm Berrigan, Chris Carosi, Patrick James Dunagan, Lawrence Ferlinghetti, Bob Holman, Andrew Joron, Elaine Katzenberger, Tim Keane, Stacy Lewis, Christophe Lima, Helen Lima, Matthew Lima, Filip Marinovich, Julio Marzán, Urayoán Noel, Arlo Quint, Ron Padgett, Guillermo Parra, Jacques Pepin, Nancy Joyce Peters, Paul Pines, Gabriella Pires, Linda Ronan, David Shapiro, Don Share, Stacy Szymaszek, Tony Towle, Nick Whittington, Wendy Xu, and, as always, the entire gang at City Lights Books.

Some of the poems appeared in *Amerarcana*, *New York Nights*, *Poetry*, and *6x6*. A shortened version of the introduction appeared in *Poetry*. The Appendix by David Shapiro first appeared as the introduction of *Inventory: New & Selected Poems* by Frank Lima (Hard Press, 1997).

FROM

Inventory: Poems

(1964)

Mom I'm All Screwed Up

Moth-eyed
          by the neon sign
                    I peeped
          at the stiff little worms
                    screwing in your head
                    spider crabs
                              crawled in my ear

With popping antennae ringlets
                    you looked like
                              a praying mantis
                    cold cream & turban
                              science fiction gleam
          as real
     as cancer
          spreading
          stuffed-tits-and-rag-guts
                    yawning
                              brillo-crotch
                    that stunk
                              all over me
          playing
                    Johnny-on-the-pony
                    on me
                              indoors

The mattress groaned
                    I moaned
          Mom
                    I'm no horse
                              you have pimples on your butt
                              your bellybutton droops

your boy-pop left
the rose of your hopes
no
no

With lollipop-grin lips
on my solitaire piece
you had no teeth
I'm still scaling scabs of
hot garlic
slob-kisses
isn't mamacita's heart going to
kiss mom
good night
no
no
no.

Mulatta

To Phyllis

And if I love you, we'll fight.
    I'll call you bitch, tack head,
And curse the gods, Lincoln, and the feminists.
Beat you—not too hard, in the right places—
    Stuff, I'm a man, no trick!
Laugh. When you cry like a child, hurt . . .
Bite, swallow the lump in my throat.
Leave,
    Take the money,
Get my belly full of cheap gin & beer;
Head full of good smoke next to a
Greasy, grinny, lip-stick whore with
    Endless, sympathetic: hum-hum, definitely,
    You're right, baby—
    Amid the gluey mist of reefer,
Cigarette and stale-green cigars,
In bar grey with the laughter of
    Hustlers, junkies, and steady, stink-finger tricks
    Where the sting-scream of the juke-box
Swells the air and makes my brain thick
    With forget-you
    And then,
The scent of your hair, body,
    When you finished cleaning the house—
Gee, I found it so delightfully unpleasant,
Sends the blood screaming through my legs for you,
And explodes the tingling blue bubble I'm in . . .
Homesickness of you begins to seep in,
    Slowly, cruelly till night skulks away

From sour, headachey dawn,
    And if I love you,
I'll wait and beat the ancient seconds of
    Without-you-since-yesterday,
As I stumble, back-bent, fumbling for keys,
Chewing Juicy Fruit,
    Up the squeaky stair, just to drown you,
    Just once more,
    In an ocean of fresh new
    I'm sorries—baby—darling—honey—please
    And hungry, stale-smoke-liquor kisses,
Gaudy, alien perfumed hugs.
And if I love you, the bitch-hate storm
Passes to the crisp white lap of
    Sheets and pillows,
Where I wander in—up—out—down
    The chestnut thighbone avenue,
Barely touching, panting, my nostrils
    Blowing
On your softsilk body to mine,
A cherry-nostrum wonder—
Experience . . .
                BANG!
. . . And if I love you, we'll fight again.

Inventory—To 100th Street

To John Bernard Myers

In the corner lot
   where they parked
         green banana trucks
       fruits
           palmed in paper straw
I smell
       bedbug & kitchen-cockroach
            summer afternoons

Somewhere
    tailless
        one-eyed cats
   doting in fat garbage cans
       screaming with the stench
   of rice & beans
         strawberry tampax
     piled
      high as the smell
       (I was small & slick)
   the covers tilted
       like the hat of a rock-look wino
           in a deep
             knee-bend nod
       on a beer
          can-street
            Sunday morning

There were always
                       time-thick
                           empty nights
         of nothing to do
                         but listen to the
  ethereal
                 (she lived on the top floor)
      I-go-for-more screams
           of Charlie's pimp's woman
               when he beat her
      for his good
            business principles
      joy-pop the block
             with morning-talk

I hear the dim iron dawn yawning
          (I lived on Third Ave.)
   rattle
      nights into
         Saturday morning
    flag-bloomer
       eclipses
just before the hunt—
     they were as big—
       the cats
   like jungle bunnies
     fierce with fleas & sores

I see window-people
     hanging out of gooey-stick slips
         sweating
         strange
  below-the-button drawers
     crouched junkies in hallways

with monkey backs
eating cellophane bananas
on a g-string
waiting
for that last bust
Spics with cock-comb
hair fronts
ear-gulping mambo music
eye-lapping pepperican flower
crotches

I can hear the streets whispering
in the ears of yelping kids

in the fun-gushing that
rippled my blood
in the pump

but the kids
are dying in the lot
like the tarry-blown feet
of the rain
jingling
on the rusty-green
of yesterday's
fire-escapes.

The Memory of Benny (Kid) Paret

To Norman & Cary Bluhm

1

Twelve Bells
   Benny's on the ropes
Twelve Bells
   he has no feet
Twelve Bells
   he can't make gloves
Twelve Bells
   one rope through his head
Twelve Bells
   one rope through his chest
Twelve Bells
   one rope through his leg
Twelve Bells
   a black pig on three spits
Twelve Bells
   a rubber apple in his mouth
Twelve Bells
   his jaw hangs like a moth
Twelve Bells
   his face is a torn flower
Twelve Bells
   his hands fall off the clocks
Twelve Bells
   he's a fly in a glass of milk.

2

Little Benny's tears
        wounded pebbles on the
                coffin lids
    your folded hands
      two dead countries
          in my head
  the rope burns
      cold welts on your back
your head is a turban
         of bandages
your eyes are bread
    I can't eat
the ring is a crib
      where you sleep
Benny's an empty bag.

Primavera

A mummy
    crumbling
        in the bar

my eyes
    empty mirrors
        my kidneys
            drunken flowers

Then dawn
    an eyelid

                                        I come to you
                                            as always

    green
            tired
                need a shave
                    a bath
                    I stink
        unlock the nights
                in jail
        it's spring on the windows
my heart
    in a bag
        and some beer

                        Hi Monkey
                        I'm home

Pudgy

I'd swish through the door
    tiptoeing
        goofed on speedballs
            with a yellow-jaundice twinkle
          in my glassy eyes

     you'd be waiting in the kitchen
      perched on a chair
       like Judge Leibowitz
        your face mooned
         wet thighs
              at me

Instead
     I'd stash my joints
      in the foodbare freezer
     take five
       throw off my clothes
      drop in bed
        like an empty pebble

I'd stink of
      catting on roofs & in basements
      barnacled with sores & pimples
       sweat-starchy socks & greasy underwear
       on my back two weeks
    you looking top-flight
    curlicues of perfume
    running through your
           nesty hair
   but I was slimming-off
      in sleep

a glazed tear on your chubby cheek
    whimpering out
                        I found a bag of that stuff
                        in the Bible—
                        you're never home anymore
   aaahhh
         shut up—
                   you're lucky I'm home tonight
and nod back in my bucket
    till the monkey
        creaked my back awake—
           gobble out of bed
              fireman my clothes on
                pistoled out of the house
   after I'd beat you out of your
    carfare & lunch money
      for my morning fix

I took cures & cures
    wrote you letters

        we'll start all over
           never take off again
             clean up for good this trip
           you were my first high
               cop a slave & work for you only
       I'm really getting down in therapy
                    this time

        sign them
             Your forever
             Loving husband

P.S. I need commissary

on a paper napkin
you wrote
Dear Liar
Come home.

O my chocolate princess
I lay in bed
smelling of Lifebuoy soap & toothpaste
light a stogie & watch the smoke
unshoe ghost-nude thoughts

my feet gag my heart
they're cold.

Abuela's Wake

Then her mouth flew open
    like a fish sucking air
        Jesus flipped with a greasy hook
I wanted to pop a cap in his plaster head

Abuelo laid with her
        naked
    he blew his nose
     his eyes
        broken toys
   while he sang her to sleep

        I'll tie your cold finger with
        ribbons for the wedding ring—
        I sold your teeth when I was drunk
        Negra Bird-Lips   my heart   your grave . . .

His lips fumbled on her wrinkled breasts
   Mom screamed barbed wire
      in my shoe-high ears
my stickball smile fell off my face

Concha
   the wake's witch
    wearing her mothball smile
    held the black rosary
     like a snake with a Catholic head
        it still hisses in my bed
   dribbling the wooden words

outside
    the snow-mouth of December tinked on the windows

By the stumped candles
    ice-bird white tearing wax
       Abuelo pillowed her head
         in the mouse-velvet coffin
           smeared her chalk face with
             glass kisses & drunk tears
      the wreaths were shadows
           standing in the corners

Abuelo sits in the kitchen
    Abuela's eyes are berries in his head
       he drinks her face in Gallo wine
         it licks his heart
           by the wedding picture
      in the empty bedroom

Abuelo
      her eyes are pools the rain can't find
        she sleeps in a green gown of moss
         and tiny paws of dew dress the grave

      your heart's a tin cup
           begging for wine.

Ventriloquist

(1967)

by Frank Lima and Joe Brainard

Underground with the Oriole

(1971)

Beach

There
        happy as a greenfly
            toes popping out
                like corks in the sand
                    Buddhas on stilted chairs
                        ocean tattooed with
                                bathing caps
                    mud castles
                                seashell windows
                and sunglasses staring
                            at the panty-blue sky
webbed seaweed
                windblown
    brown
                on an eel-green
                                        bottle

On the meat line
        sun sprays of iodine
            on fish-white backs
                    wide splits
                            heavy squats with cat whiskers
I'm the ocean between their legs
                my toetips cling to the seashore
                        sea gulls whirlpool in my hair
                            and sing in my windy ear
O beach
        heaven of dark-eyed belly buttons
            you tricked-off the seashell
                    for Trojan-floats & beer cans.

Haiku

For Frank O'Hara

I
The lights are out
The cats are hungry
The room is full of gangsters

II
The dishes are dirty
The icebox is empty
I dream of celery and a compass

III
The roof is upstairs
The window next door
A guitar in the shower

IV
The hours disappear in my room
Where is my blue pistol
The door-god is knocking.

The Woman

Today I met my woman in the subway . . . it was winter.
She wore a red coat down to her knees with a black
fur collar. I could only see the back of her head,
which was blue because of the kerchief & the flower
she wore. She wasn't facing me. Her shoes were
orange and her stockings black. I went up to her
and said I had found a little part of her in all
the women I had ever known, and I had always loved her.
I told her: "We can make it & crib together . . .
Things won't be too bad . . . life is a snap!"

Then she turned to me. Her face was sea-brown; her
lips were thick; her eyes were dried wells and the
flower in her hair was plastic. I said to her that
I loved her more than ever now and must know her name
because she was what life was about. She grinned:
her teeth were stubs of jade. I kissed her and sucked
her lips. She said any name would do. . . . I called her
My Woman and I took her hand. It was like old dried
wood with cracks in it; her knuckles were cold lumps
I pressed to my face.

She unbuttoned her coat. Her body was black and her skin
was wrinkled and stuck to her bones like tape. She had
no breasts; they were eaten away by cancer I guess.
My hands were filled with warm and slippery flesh.

She kicked off her orange shoes and asked me to kiss
her feet . . . they were small and her toes were chewed
stubs. I said I would kiss them if only she would give

me her heart. She said she would in exchange for mine. I told her my heart was young and full, filled with flowers, birds and perfumed tears, but if she wanted it she could have it.

The train came to a sudden stop. It was spring. I fell away from her across the aisle dreaming of wreaths. She dropped her heart and kicked it over to me. I took it . . . it was a coffin filled with dry worms. I ran off with it, as happy as a faggot in boy's town.

Submarine

I cannot feel her voice I am too far away skiing in Austria.
Perhaps I will go to another country disguised as frozen gas
And travel beneath her skirt into the center of the earth.
I have an air bubble in my ear that needs light.
It is yellow and I slip over the lintel to correct the sun.

Here is a white charm. My hand cannot hold it.
The stars are lost and the birds have absorbed the wind.
It doesn't matter I am going mad listening to the noises—
The young girls on the waves. They are white like telephones.
My arms are tired and they will not let me go because I refuse
To undress them without passionate words.

Acid

through a hole in my hand
I have your face in my hand
I have a knife on the ceiling
To fly through the ceiling
Like a knife in your room
I kill the walls in your room
While the dead women sleep
We smoke through the walls
We inhale the walls
Our bodies are beautiful
They are numbers in our throats.

Poem

Tomorrow
I'll go
Fishing
On the
Ganges
With an
Orange
Some rice
And gather
My hands
Then I'll
Entreat
Your window
On a scaffold
In September
I'll hide
In your
Shower
Because
I am also
A philosopher

Underground with the Oriole

To Joe and Rosemary

I have been bled
Twice this year . . .
But I can see the workers,
They are like stones that keep the sky in place.
The weather is like the sky,
The arch of heaven with incredible weight,
With a blue curve that does not let me sleep.

Below us the bathers wade in rings of water:
And it is April as we leave the room with a glass of music,
Judging my footsteps carefully.
The soles of my feet are Greece,
And I have a beautiful wind.

The oil in the sand reminds me of paradise.
I wish I were underground with the oriole:
I would wear a bronze mask and give you my silver,
My accounts and my green vestments
So no one would pass or hesitate at your figure,
The figure of a sea horse.

In the air lovers are whispering to each other,
They believe in mirages and paper formulas.
In Asia the dispute for ashes has begun:
The itchy substance for allegory
Where the stones lie by the water in a trance.
I have been here seven years pretending
To go mad on a bed of fire,
But rains are imminent this year.

It is Sunday in the huge glass house
As we descend the stairs to lay the flowers by the sea—
Suddenly the man with the watch is overwhelmed,
By the fog,
It was beautiful the clear silhouette of her body
In the deserted streets,
As though the atmosphere had lost its way
In the frantic upheaval of the crowds.

My skin has grown tighter from the strain,
I'm no longer in radiant health,
There is an epidemic raging in me:
I am afraid of birds.
A cold blast of air has hit my stomach!
Was it an earthquake?   Or an approaching storm?

The crossing was very difficult.
The light was pink on the foam of the crashing waves.
They glowed like coils with ruffles on the edges.
On the bottom the seaweed moved carefully
In a desert on a soft night
As the moon turned toward the wall.

I came away from the crowd seasick:
Each summer I have lost a wife in this room—
I tighten the bed with winter and prepare for disease
And rub my body with alum and water
Knowing I will drown in the undercurrent
With the forms on the ceiling and the ladder pointing
Toward the window.

summer   (a love poem)

I wanted to be sure this was our island
so we could walk between the long stars by the sea
though your hips are slight and caught in the air
like a moth at the end of a river around my arms
I am unable to understand the sun your dizzy spells
when you form a hand around me on the sand

I offer you my terrible sanity
the eternal voice that keeps me from reaching you
though we are close to each other every autumn
I feel the desperation of a giant freezing in cement
when I touch the door you're pressed against
the color of your letter that reminds me of flamingos

isn't that what you mean?
the pleasure of hands and
lips wetter than the ocean
or the brilliant pain of
breathless teeth in a
turbulent dream on a roof
while I thought of nothing
else except you against
the sky as I unfolded you
like my very life a liquid
signal of enormous love we
invented like a comet that
splits the air between us!

the earth looks shiny wrapped in steam and ermine
tired of us perspiring at every chance on the floor
below I bring you an ash tray out of love for the
ice palace because it is the end of summer the end

of the sun because you are in season like a blue
rug you are my favorite violin when you sit and
peel my eyes with your great surfaces seem intimate
when we merely touch the thread of life and kiss

7.30.69

Ode to Love

My island is trouble:
I have found wet grass in my armpits
and yellow paint in my navel since you left

Do you believe in a cold sane reality?
love is love like a mountain in the room
with a common cold so take my head
I am a wandering snowshoe at your feet

I cannot sleep there is sand in my shoes
there is a wine spot in my dreams that makes me dizzy
I feel like a cloud in the Pacific Ocean stunned by the weather
like an old cover on a new book in your hands
if I were a fur coat you could not get me off in case of fire
I'm interested in the finer things in life like swimming to Australia
in a heat wave in my arms with only salt between us
we will stop smoking for days on end in our journey
you make me restless when you use up all the air around us
I feel like a gorilla in a chocolate shower
when we watch the sun go down for the last time
if I were lost on this island I would send you my
heart on a raft with some lunch and a love letter:

"My Dearest I am lost."

I am needed here like the sky needs air traffic therefore
I am bored with the idea of life without you on this planet
I want you to be my room deodorant my favorite stone
O ship of love I wish you would blow up when I think of
internal motivation I think of my liver on rainy days when it hurts
poets are really nice people they're like giant trees
full of sap!

O sun sun my life has not been a drag after all
I could have been a number in a marble game

When I think of you I can spare myself from sleep
I can be as loyal as Blue Cross and as silly as this poem
I am killing my ash tray with an overdose of butts
when I talk to my ash tray about you it gets bored
my subjects are monotonous so it tells me
That's life ash tray.

I will wrap myself in toothpaste every morning and bring
you your favorite coffee for I will be your cup
how can I become famous when I am so distracted?

There is a tiny creep in the room that steals my cigarettes
I won't kill him because I'm in love and nothing else matters
but love on this gorgeous Earth that we're on this wonderful trap
Anyhow I feel like an overcrowded greenhouse when you're around.

Ode to Love—Part 2

(litany)

"I am alone in New York I am the mud
from heaven I have distracted this
society with the filth of my life
I have pumped and polluted the streets
with my determinations I have willed
my will with a monotonous infamy
Destroy yourself if you don't know!
I speak from a terrible inner place
before the beginning of my birth
I have been the unnatural vigor of
dreams the meditations of the insane
and the model of the dead my dreams
are countries in another city in hotels
with solitary radios with eyelids and
lipstick on the thread of life for a
dollar I have slaughtered my loins for
a fake and for the scandal in my body
in pursuit of love and my life I take
this for myself with no qualms with no
discretion for I do not fear my blood
any longer or the minerals in my body
before an instant death surrounded by
criticism and chaos waiting for a final
star in a room for a glittering tear on
the floor the color of heaven for I have
been my own somnambulist saint the invention
of my nerves love has been a temporary lift
from nostrils and navel-sucking and from the

petty boredom of a hot body around the channels
of my waist in some emergency!"   O fuck who cares.

But it is Sunday and I have come through without a scratch
or a watch to tell you of that time or anyone for that
matter my excitement is your short black hair lighting your
cigarettes over a dinner table or holding your hand in the
theater or saying nothing when we're together on an island
on a magic ocean in the mornings.

This is what I have my new life and a beach full of cabbage
so we can be alone in this mad world of silly images I
promise you 80 years more of life because I feel like a
watermelon covered with Jergens Lotion!   I am mad to think
these things but it is a good and kindly madness that will
do the world some good.

I have lived with a broken heart since I can remember since
Webster wrote his wonderful book to Mary if I stop writing
I'll go out like a light and wake up in another marathon
or another life dreaming of you I need coffee.
Someone has put a hand in my coffee if it were yours I don't
think I would stir it for fear of dying of my own perspiration
if you suddenly appeared in my room nude how would you go back
if I drank coffee? That's life baby.

Men cry because they do not have the will to live I wonder if
living is a sideline if you're not in love? I wonder about a
lot of things like how you take a shower how you grin when you
brush your teeth how you feel when you think of me as the only
man in the world like me?

Well the time has come to clip my nails and play one last
piece and settle with the Earth for a night and a token of
love your love and the nourishment of a dream with you your
eyes like growing flowers your flowers the vegetation of
Spain a great sadness if you will it on the world.

Sunday, 9.7.69

morning   sara

toward the end you are sunburned
and I am a blister if only I weren't
human I would throw you out with
great passion no excuses just love
for your own good—

you shit!   you're late!

since I have nothing better to do
let me watch you piss and I will
excuse you from the world
call you lake or long-leg-waterfall
I am hungry and go thru your underwear

give me some hot soup or
I'll suck on the curtains!

would you like an omelette
with diced candles and mushrooms?
or a garbage truck in an opera?
do you put lipstick on your nipples?
I'd like to think so your body like
the streets in Amsterdam the harbor
in your hair the canals down your
back in the mornings as I sweep the
flowers off you when the alarm goes
off I wake up like a net fumbling for love

so pull me close to you
and strike the morning ice

and I will gather myself up
from the filth of dreams
shave shower and kiss you!

East 5th Street, 7.7.70

FROM

Angel

(1976)

159 John Street

It will rain forever here
the buildings will be turned down
the artist will obscure the weather
the potters and the weavers
will rub the edges of the sand and
a wolf will come to the door
to explain the facts of my life

without illusion our jaws will lock
because it is a common attitude

when you limp
I think of your waterfall larger
than my birth

there are no essentials
about my life
the doctor was ugly
and the nurses were beautiful
a myth to the contrary is a lie.

Natasha

To My Daughter

When your tongue slipped into the world
like a drop of light I thought of mirrors
and the fantasy of numbers

If the world would change
we could take our clothes off
and allow each other the words
of a whore in love with her reflections

I follow my delirium from room
to room and I am cured of life
like the thinker of fire
the father of all liquids.

Hart's Island

I write this to you
from the giant's head.

The beetles move in my
cell telling me of your
shape and your walk
and I accuse them of forgery.

They think they know the
outline of my thoughts,
they do not know the terror
in my face, the evidences of waste.

Perhaps my shoulders could
tell you where I have been all
these years, in another universe,
on the carpet of summer
offering a new life to flies.

Hunter Mountain

The sky has the luxury of going anywhere.
The roads follow with the
gratitude of being abandoned
and watch the deer run through smoke.

This is the day of the animals' feeding on our waste,
the fatality of hands passing a soft spot,
the heavy breathing of small yellow animals.
This is my infancy:
three hours from New York,
a fall flexing of odors,
the desperate hunger in a car that sucks the air.

The expectancy of a garden full of wolves,
the face of a tiger in an ashtray.
I move and lie against someone
and plant light where I am correct.

This is the perfect place.
My children spin like bottles
because I am able to lie.
l smile in terror when they touch me.
The facts of my life remain facts.

I offer the guest no memories, no seasons.
The rusted cities of the sea gulls wash ashore
in some cocktail party like a large bird.

Have I stood over you with yellow eyes?
I was prowling your stark white floors at the bottom of the cage
with such brilliance that I have given up sleep.

I have run through my lungs
down down down into the water
where the fish bring light to the sun
waiting for the weakness of a dreamer.

Soliloquy

The final creatures decide if we're suitable for breathing
In this new life wolves watch the spots we leave behind
But I can swim through concrete
It's easy, walk into my cage and ask the lions
Why they smell like money
Ask them why the streets limp when you walk them
Night is the time of the limpers
They cover the rocks in the bars
The limpers are at the end of the street waiting
To catch the city like a bird
It's the night of the limpers
They follow me home like a hangover
You can limp to the end of the world
I'll wait for you in the alley
You are on my back like the smoke of a .38 special
It's noon in the shovel I'm holding
I'm looking for your neck
I know the worms are hiding the pearls.

Lobster

For Esti Dunow

The Maine lobster is the most famous of all the shellfish. These creatures gave birth to an extraordinary planet that was able to produce one million different species of lobsters and 350,000 different kinds of humans. The lobster lives and dies, struggles and adapts, and all the while deepens the ocean to preserve the imagination of the universe:

> perhaps some ten billion light-years away,
> when comets were flies, supernovae frogs,
> the galaxies were born; and in this tiny speck
> the dream of this crustacean was a strange,
> wonderful, and improbable eater.

So cold was the dream in spots that the temperatures plunged to –140°F and the iciest lobster grew 9,200 feet thick. So warm was the dream that the temperature reached 138° in the shade where it flourished at depths of six miles, before the eaters moved onto the land.

The lobsters grew wings, making possible a variety of vegetation from tiny flowers to massive woods that resisted the face of the earth. And in one of nature's most amazing creations, the lobsters stepped out of the shower dripping wet and into the machines that move at the bottom of the sea, where they beat each other with bay leaves, vinegar, and wine.

Lobsters are like old men in the bathhouses who dream of Vulcan and varicose veins. The lobsters appear to be hot balloons that frighten the kiss of death. But they know the kiss of death is going bald in fine restaurants: and one can notice, just off center, the fine white laugh of the lobster.

The Underworld

This beautifully marked insect has a bright yellow body with black wings and a forehead. It sings clear and strong but can no longer fly in a smooth pattern near the ground. In the spring it goes unmarked and pale blue. It ranks high among men and is malodorous and reddish as were the stone men. During the war there was a bizarre incident: The idea was that the insects would transmit the yips of enemy soldiers. The plan was fascinating but had to be abandoned.

This insect is possessed of sexual powers, and the typical male copulates at dawn in every way possible. The male comes near a couple who are mating and he becomes terribly excited. He punctures the abdomen of the female. This development has no reason. In fact, they have no limits of irregularity. But the African species are developing facial muscles that indicate emotions.

from "Dracula to the Angels"

As a result of spring the mosquitoes are magnificent.
From the point of view of the air they are unfathomable.
—we don't deserve them—

Mosquitoes are accustomed to considering themselves perfect.
This year they will withdraw
With a mouthful of poets.
Poets are to mosquitoes what cigarettes are to lung cancer:
There are too many poets and not enough mosquitoes.
To the mosquitoes it's a matter of survival:

1. a poet sees an owl and he thinks of a woman's crotch—
2. a mosquito sees a poet and he thinks of a woman's crotch—

Poets and mosquitoes have on thing in common—
They suck.

el Bronx

I hate the Orient in the morning. The kisses are too slow, like the breaking of smallpox and the women who have three tits struggle from one continent to another:

Everything trembles in this building when the lovers fuck. They think they're putting the salt back in the sand. And the tenants wonder about the dogs at dawn that rest like the wind on a gleaming taxi. Why should I leave this swamp? The showers are relentless, and the water is always hot, as hot as the three small closets that we have full of shoes worshipping the small clouds of underwear, the butterflies of smoke.

The Turtles of the Bronx

Roberta floats in silence across the kitchen
squeezing lumps of boredom into ice. Her mother's
house lies frozen in the Bronx delighted by the

organs left behind: six living pregnancies conceived
by the Milky Way and with the proper things to eat.
Her father's leftovers acquired the sponginess of

life, because mankind is doomed if you don't
scream at night. O night, the spies of the stars were
fragile just before they took off their shoes.

Scenario

For Edwin Denby

The curtain rises and the stage is dark. An alarm clock is heard and the stage becomes brightly lit. The stage is divided.

STAGE RIGHT
A huge alarm clock is seen, a huge bed, chair and full-length mirror, and other large objects that are found in a bedroom. There is a figure in the bed.

STAGE LEFT
A dance studio with mirrors in the background and life-size or larger-than-life sculptures or paintings of legendary great dancers. Young dancers, wearing brightly colored leotards, are frozen in a tableau.

THE DANCE

EPISODE I
Edwin cheerfully bounces out of bed wearing a pale raincoat. He dances around the bed, the clock, and the other large objects in the room as if to greet them, ending in front of the mirror where he strikes the exaggerated poses of a fashion model. He gracefully takes off the raincoat, throws it on a chair and then stretches many times. He holds his hands up to the mirror and examines them carefully, revolving them in the air like an Indian dancer.

EPISODE II
While Edwin is examining his hands, the dance students suddenly come to life with quick, erratic, jerky motions. Edwin enters the studio and with a sweep of his hands stops what they are doing and gently admonishes them. He proceeds to teach them the

formal dance. He shows them various steps and stances, but never gives them the opportunity to follow any of his examples. Instead he dances and dances around them, and the dance students mock him by bowing and clapping politely. They thank him and he dismisses them. They leave. Edwin is bewildered and sad as he returns to his room. He walks to the mirror, holds his hands up and examines them carefully, revolving them in the air like an Indian dancer.

EPISODE III

As Edwin enters his room, the lights are dimmed and a young couple enter the studio furtively. They are wearing pale raincoats. The young man takes his raincoat off and then takes the raincoat off the young girl. At this moment, Edwin takes the raincoat off an imaginary dancer in his room. The young couple begin to dance. Edwin dances with his invisible partner doing the same dance. The young couple stop. Edwin stops. The young man takes his raincoat and drapes it on his and her shoulders; simultaneously, Edwin puts his raincoat on. The lights become dimmer as the young couple kiss and leave the stage. Edwin goes to bed.

CURTAIN

Cuachtemoc

This knife is as long as my wife in the pool
and I am as dark as the sun
The silence from the moon is as dark when we sleep

I always bring my captives here
and let the grapevines choke them

The stars will crash and last for years
I grin at them and give them fruit
I am an expert at my job
I am their home

I spend the morning writing letters
while the machines crush the priest
I remember their flat runways
when they stripped for weddings

It was the death of all the warriors
and their enemies
When the wind screamed around their feet
I would listen to my knife

It was the time to pull their hearts out
and give them to the children

I have given them the wings to heaven
and they are my last legend
frozen like the hands of a small monkey

We call their last sounds the wind
This sound brings us childhood

as if it were life
These are the days of our calendar

Our children pray to them
and play with their hearts with sticks
We pray to the children and their sticks
and it rains for hours on the crops

Lightning makes the trees smell like my knife
As long as the heart is quiet we are waterproof

I am the king of the shade in the green jungle
The people hurry to see my accidents
The mothers among them hold their children up to me
Their small bones make very little noise

They exchange gifts
Some of them have not seen
each other since the last rain.

Ochun

These long roads to the moon are the bits of scorpion
that are left on the way
like a tent around my neck
the day my skin pealed
like the songs in my mother's hand.

My father read the future in the mountains
under their platinum skin
the blue gas was as gentle as
the dialogue of an ostrich
and his obsessive kindness
the slow oars of the stars
a diamond waiting for a house
the astounding darkness around my brother's daughter
the horrible green
the purple lips of a choir.

Plena

During the day I play at drowning
looking for the smoke
of eyelashes and faded hair
the lilac shadows of blood
and the ruins of coffee
but at night
I dream of the last syllable
in my mother's heart
the last red word in her lungs.

FROM

Inventory: New & Selected Poems

(1997)

Scattered Vignettes

I remember what I remember
I remember writing a poem
About me
About you
About the Christ
About the thing in the garden:

We were stars in my mother's belly.
We were the faces of the angels;
like the angels we came into this world
with blood on our wings.

The angels are God's hit squad:
Whenever He wanted someone assassinated,
He sent an angel to do His dirty work:
Sodom and Gomorrah.
The angels always smell
like fine cigars.

My father's mother was a poor Indian who made
and sold confections in the streets
of Guadalajara to make ends meet.
The town doctor was
Don Francisco Lima,
of Castilian descent
and my grandmother,
Benigna's, paramour.

Don Francisco died when my father was very young.
My grandmother
armed herself with a gun

and took my father to the
funeral to see his father for the last time.

This was scandalous to
Don Francisco's grieving family,
and his practice which was the entire town.

As a boy I imagined my grandmother
stepping out of a Paul Muni cloud of dust
with a long barreled gun in one hand
and this filthy neonate in tow in the other hand.

The white European-descent-small-Mexican-town aristocracy
must have shit in their white stucco catholic church!

My father would relate these events to me
while at the kitchen table,
in tears,
between drinks on his only day off.
When my father spoke of his childhood
in Mexico,
I could hear the mariachis singing
"La Paloma" in the background
and see the white dove on the windowsill.

One hot, dry day after the funeral my grandmother,
accompanied by my father, was selling her candies
when she was approached by a young man on horseback
who turned out to be my father's half brother.

He was abusive to my father's mother.
Why else
would one hack his own half brother to death?

My father fled the country.
He was wanted for murder.
The story got murky.
My father was drunk and pissing in his pants.

I don't remember him ever vomiting;
he was a real pro.

Anyway,
he became a romantic fugitive
bumming around the country eating raw potatoes,
iguanas (the Mexican walking lunch)
and hiding in abandoned barns and farm houses.

He finally made his way east to Veracruz
where he boarded a merchant ship bound for Europe.
He was a stowaway.

His tale of survival was permeated with spirits
and machismo.
He hid in a coal bin
and ate whatever moved within his reach.
He was discovered by a stoker
who took pity on his emaciated
and filthy condition.
This chthonic creature
from the bowels of the ship
saved my father's life
by sharing stale bread
and rotten vegetables with him.

My father was convinced
the stoker
was not what he appeared to be.

He was the *vision serpent* sent
by his forefathers to rescue him:

      the stoker's aspect would change
      from a man to an animal:
      sometimes he appeared before my
      father as a bat with bread
      as a snake with water or
      when my father was homesick
      and missed his mother
      the stoker would appear
      as a spider with sugar

My father was not afraid of the dark.
It was its vastness
and lack of sunlight
that my father found foreboding and ominous.

In the immensity of that metal darkness
he would cry for the sun to appear
and blind his mind of all memory:

  his tears were
    tiny glass scorpions
      tumbling from his face,
        shattering on the floor
          forming little pools
            of light

The soot-covered wingless angel
of mercy never betrayed my father's
whereabouts to anyone onboard ship.
My father expressed these events
to me

with reverence
as if he were reciting
a long forgotten prayer.
Although he was frozen and silent,
I imagined his eyes
were speaking to me
and divulging secret adventures
that I would
understand when I got older.
Perhaps even undertake myself.

My father never spoke to me
or my brothers while he was sober.
He was proud of the scars on his face
and a bullet embedded in his back
that looked like a baby trying to escape
from a flaccid marshmallow Easter egg.

He never played with us or touched us
except when he was drunk.
On Sunday mornings he would wake us up:
He would be wearing my mother's negligee,
her bra, exaggerated makeup and sloppy lipstick.

He would come into our beds to roughhouse with us.
Through my mother's nightgown I could see
and feel the hair on his body,
like chicken wire covered with velvet.

On Sunday mornings I attended mass at Saint Cecilia's
Roman Catholic church with my grandmother,
Dolores, which is plural for pain: Many pains.
She was my mother's mother.

I was an altar boy
in the service of the church
and the almighty Father Archangel
who perspired a lot no matter what the weather was.
A pious man whose gullet
was the ciborium of the
sacred blood of Christ:
Each day,
at dusk,
Father Archangel was in a
sublunary alcoholic fog,
stumbling and grunting in the sacristy,
shooing away the floating angels
he had disgorged into the piscina.

He was often hungover and irritable
the following day and acted as if
he had survived a meaningless war
where he had lost every thing,
his biretta,
his immortal soul.

He would be out of spiritual breath
as he climbed out of his wine-colored pit.
During these humane interludes,
he would often speak to me
in quiet tones about the priesthood
and its burdens.

One such burden was his erotic dreams
and the torments he suffered
when he had an erection.
He would ask me if I,
at my age,

had erotic dreams and erections.
He would never let me answer the questions,
and interject, reassuringly,
that it was natural and physical.

I knew at that instance he had another
ecclesiastical attack of libidinal repentance.
What is the act of contrition
for a twelve year old priest-fucker?

I thought,
how can I get kicked out of the mother church?
Get excommunicated!
In those days there was no such thing
as ratting-out an aging,
fag priest.

It came to me in a walking dream
on my way home from school:
Saturday night when everyone was asleep
I took my mother's Alka-Seltzer
from the medicine cabinet,
unwrapped them carefully
and placed them in a napkin in my
Sunday-pants' pocket.
Sunday morning before mass
I very carefully substituted
the holy wafers with the Alka-Seltzer.
I arranged them in such a way
that every other person would receive
one Alka-Seltzer.

I felt an extraordinary feeling of accomplishment
and genius for someone who could not read the word "the".

At the same time I was petrified with fear;
my legs were weak and would not carry me.
It was going to be the end of the world.

The Daily News would carry the story
when the smoked cleared
and they found my beige body.

That was wishful thinking.
The big white finger in the sky
would get me first and drill me
like a gimlet right into hell!

Maybe I could cut a deal with the devil and paint signs for him.
It was the only thing I did well in school.
Maybe I could learn to read in hell.
Anyway, I would get there before Father Archangel
and whack him since I was already in hell.

The eucharistic rite was in slow motion:
Father Archangel was shining and white,
floating in the air as he performed the rites.
My feeling was he knew what was going to happen
and deliberately let it happen in order to become
a martyr and a saint.

There were millions of expectant parishioners
in the church that morning.
Saint Cecilias,
a church no bigger than a house fly,
in the village of Spanish Harlem,
had miraculously become a gigantic cathedral that morning
because it knew that an extraordinary event would take place
and that I was responsible.

Then everything stopped moving
except for Archangel's hands
inserting the holy wafer
into the open mouths of the expectant parishioners
that instantly erupted belching white foamy lava.

They were like mad dogs foaming at the mouth
and barking at the oblivious priest
as he held the apocryphal Grail up to heaven
offering my beige body,
my blood
to Jesus Christ.
He screamed!

And I disappeared
into a long puff
of marijuana,
alcohol and drugs.

My mother is a *Santera*:
Santerismo is not witchcraft.
Witchcraft implies evil doing.
In *Santerismo*
the person who offers the service
is the belief system.
The services can bring harm to someone;
can right a wrong;
effect a cure of an illness;
attract or drive away a lover.

She employs auguries,
strange forms of phylacteries,
talismans
and all manner of potions,

including rituals for unrequited love when
menstrua occurs.

Notwithstanding,
a *Santera* is a medium,
a vessel for the spirits from heaven or hell:
These spirits would occupy my mother's body
and use her faculties to communicate with the payee.
She did well.

The procurer of my mother's services would benefit,
therefore it is not considered evil.

Only the two demons that are at the right and left
of the devil, *Altaro*, *Altaclan*, and the one in front of him,
the most malefic, *Altaru*, are evil.
Therefore, one respects the devil
as he directly does not cause evil.
Evil is the invocation and not the act of placing a glass
of clear water with a rose in it on a windowsill.

My mother would dress me up
in little girls' dresses
before I was old
enough to attend school.

She often photographed me on these occasions
and would show them to her friends with the
casualness of a reminiscing parent.
And with the manners of a pedantic official,
she would speak of me as if I were far away
attending some wonderful college.

In this tableau vivant,
my mother would mention that she always wanted a girl.
In these soft black and white photographs
I would be wearing a voluminous
white dress;
bobby socks
and buckled shoes to match;
my hair was long and curly,
and arranged in a coif of light colored ribbons.
I had a puzzled look on my face.

When I began grade school I was ashamed
to go to the boys' room with the other boys
because I was wearing little girl's underwear that were
pink and shiny.

While my father was at work,
my mother had male friends visit her.
I was forbidden to ever mention these visits to my father
or my grandparents who lived in the same building just
across the hall:

My family and my mother's family occupied the entire floor.
We were told (I have two younger brothers, Phillip and Kelly)
to stay in our room during these visitations.
I would sneak out and watch my mother engage
in acts with these men that I had witnessed the
night before while my mother and father thought
we were asleep.

I remember one of my mother's paramours in particular,
el Patilludo, the one with exaggerated sideburns.

He was always attired in black bell bottom pants and had shiny,
black mummified hair that was as sleek and tight as a shower cap
on his head and obviously attended to with laborious care.
He was taller than my mother.
I would watch: He would be kneeling in front of her
between her legs in the kitchen as that was the farthest room
and the most remote from the bedroom.

He would have tears in his eyes that accumulated
on his mustache like icicles.
My mother would lovingly,
with the tip of her tongue,
lick the tears from his eyes.

El Patilludo looked like one of the flamenco dancers
in a poster that hung in the living room.

I once overheard my mother mention that he reminded
her of Valentino, the great lover of silent films.
Yeah, right. Only if Valentino had the puffy cheeks
of a beer drinker.

My mother's lovers all had code names
as they were more often than not
the surreptitious exchange between her
and her band of house-coat-and-pin-curler friends
immediately following the departure
of one of my mother's lovers.

They were
hungry lionesses
quickly approaching
a freshly killed corpse
of gossip.

My mother was the queen bee who provided
lascivious pollen to these pedestrian drones.
The kitchen was suddenly aglow with
their shiny cold cream faces
and the hushed tones of erotic whispers;
a forum for explicit comparisons of amatory techniques
and erogenous wishful thinking as these women
were all married and would not dare cheat
on their Carlos and Fernando:
Mr. Spanish Dick, Sr.
The consequences would be
facial disfigurement
with a straight razor
or two slashes across the ass,
so she could not lay on her back
and fuck anybody else,
by a self-righteous,
jealous husband who had been
fucking anything that walked,
in the name of his manly,
macho duty because all mighty
God had given him
His only begotten twelve inch dick!

My family life came to an abrupt end
when I mentioned these events to my
grandmother who confronted my mother.
My mother became a beige tropical tower
scintillating anger who threw me out
of the house naked into the hall of
the building for betraying her.
I lived with my grandparents after that.
My mother did not speak to me for months.

At my grandparents',
I listened to the radio late into the night.
The radio was a miniature church with a green,
luminous Christ that emanated music and white,
masculine voices that told stories.

As I listened
late at night,
I ate salt from my left hand,
while turning the dial
with my right hand.
I was the only human being
alive
on the face of the earth
and I was communicating
with fantastic beings
in the green cathode night.

Eventually I returned home. My father was losing
one job after another because of his drinking.
He was hallucinating, chasing away the *vision serpent*
and becoming violent and dangerous.
When my parents separated I remember going to school
on an abandoned iceberg, not being able to read or spell
words that I could the day before for the teacher.
I wrote plays for a puppet theater I had constructed
and recited poetry from memory. All that vanished
when my father left home. Until now that has been
the most tragic event in my life.
The end came one Sunday spring afternoon
at dinner, when, what seemed, without provocation,
my father cut the left side of my mother's face.
In slow motion my brother Phillip and I beat him
with baseball bats into a pool of blood.

I had a .22 caliber automatic Italian Bareta
that I jammed in his face, cocked the trigger,
and told him to back off, to leave.

He looked at me as if he were going to tell me one last
story with his eyes once again, he smiled ever so slightly
and told my mother, without ever taking his Maya-black
eyes from me, that I would cause her the most pain and
trouble. He left and so did the Mariachis and *"La Paloma"*
on the windowsill.

One summer afternoon some of my boyhood friends told me
that their parents had seen my father on a bench on East
110th in Central Park drinking with a bunch of bums.
I don't remember walking or running to the park to see my
father. I just appeared across the street and he was there,
dirty and unshaven.

He was sitting on a bench with his arms around a woman
who was fat and as dirty as he was. There were other
derelicts on the park bench, but the woman fascinated
me for some unknown reason. Her stockings were loosely
rolled around her ankles. My father's once jet black
hair was grey and as long as the Indians' on TV.
Although it was summer he was wearing a tattered winter
coat that was many sizes too big.

He was Moses–Charlton Heston holding a pint of wine
up to the sky in one hand and the woman's hand in the other.
The bottle was the law and she was his staff.

The woman and my father were both drinking from the same
bottle as if they were sharing some spiritual part of
their lives, some mysterious part of their bodies, with

each other. There was something magical in that bottle
that bound them together. That woman and what was left of
my father would part the sea in my life forever.
I stared and did not cross the street to speak to him.
I vanished as quickly as I appeared into another puff of smoke.

I remember it was a noisy spring in Spanish Harlem when
I came home one evening after running the streets. I found
my mother in the bedroom sitting in front of her Renaissance
Bronx-Italian vanity; her face was glowing with mascara
and rouge. She was wearing large ornamental, miniature
playground-swing earrings made of gold, and all her
jewelry and her favorite perfume, FOLLOW ME: It was a
dark blue bottle with a white decal of a palm tree and
a quarter moon.

Her hair was in what she called her Joan Crawford upsweep,
held in place, in the center, by a large Spanish comb that
was flanked by two long ornate, lethal skewers.

Her eyes were puffy and moist. She looked like a
Chinese emperor with lollipops in her hair. She calmly
faced me and informed me that my father was dead.
Before I uttered a word, she became quite erect and
announced, with an air of glutinous authority,
that the cause of his death was "acute alcoholism."

She almost smiled as if the term would somehow
dignify his condition in Central Park.
As if he were a great casualty of an honorable war.

The fierce caveman in drag was dead.
The warrior who vanquished cirrhotic spirits was dead.

My mother began to drink a lot.
One summer night she was drinking and became ill.
She was glistening with perspiration,
cheap perfume and wrapped in cigarette smoke.
She asked me to help her to bed.

She was wearing a house dress with nothing underneath.
This was shortly after my father's death.
I may have been twelve,
perhaps younger.

She asked me to lie next to her.
I did and fell asleep next to her
with extraordinary anticipation.

When I awoke she was a warm mist hovering,
suspended over me,
naked,
a giant night bird
whose soft long feathers
were sweeping my body away
into the cumulus clouds
of black pubic hair.
My pants were down to my knees.
I looked at her for an instant.
A nano second in a boy's erotic time.

She was startled.
I put myself back to sleep.
No, a coma.

    the bells
  in all the children's books
    were broken

all the shooting stars fell
   out of heaven
and it was forever darkness
   and sadness
at night the moon would burn
   thereafter
   like a rose
that would always belong
   to my mother

          I had drunk
        Medusa's blood,
      in the dark,
    saw her face,
      but,
     unlike Perseus,
I became the blind groom
   of unfathomable
     fascination

After that whenever she began to drink,
I would stay home with her.
She was the moonlight.
She was the darkness.

When my boyhood friends would boast of
seeing so-and-so's panties,
I would go home to be with my mother.

My first arrest took place in junior high school:
a gun.
My second arrest:
a gun, etc.
I was in a club called

The Young Demons.
We were into guns,
drugs and territory.
My life was rehabs,
Arrests and jails
Crabs
Syphilis
Hepatitis

And finally
The mad houses:
These were the walls of insomnia
Where Dante became incontinent and feeble,
Twirling his eighteen inch Asian penis;
Where God sat in an antique electric chair
Preaching the gospel of a heaven made of iron;
Where doctors and lawyers
Burned their faces with lighted cigarettes;
Where human excrement was soap
And patients removed imaginary wires from their throats;
Where the clouds of heaven could be bought for a blow job.

In Memory of Eugene Perez

(Drowned May 25, '62)

Botchy-white balloon-blown
    like a rubber ball
  the East River coughs you up
    clutching holy sea-weed
oil-slicks halo your shriveled mouth

Eels party in the sunken sockets
      of your eyes
   crabs ear-ring your ears
your soul smells in the river
    but your heart hangs in my seclusion room
      your blobbed face won't knife your therapist's sleep
       St. Peter picks the worms
         in your feet

Turno
   you got in the wind
     I heard your lungs croak on the
      11 p.m. ebb
    while your ghost strokes
      in hell's fish bowl.

FROM

Year's End

Year's End

I
When I pause, anemones fall on the month of December.
And I am foolish enough to answer the phone, like a drop
of water sliding across a linen tablecloth, falling
on the lap of a lover. I have,
in my hand, the channel of sovereign energy, the quiet
continent that hardens into soil. A fine Minnesota rain
falls on the swans that have given their wet bread to
the enemy in the pool. What shall I bring tomorrow?

II
Nature's caricatures have left us the tender sounds
of a throat in mourning for the throbbing of the Earth.
So we ascend through our afflictions to catch a fleeing
thought, the loveliest of the airs between us. A hand is lost
in the Oblivion. How many thoughts does it take to make
a century? Life, with all its evenings,
religiously returns each morning like
a mountain opening up within the heart.

III
I suspect when I pause on the month of December
anemones fall.
Dear sacred heart, each Friday I crawl away from your soft
leather orchid that shatters my soul with its dark
shudders of moonlight.

The History of Night

Night falls at different speeds and at the center
there are drops of rain. Not far from
the bed meteorites
thinly coat the entire universe.
The zodiac floats into icicles that form
our passing glances.
Should the sun throw more light on glimmering
autumn, the leaves would
shut our arms that dangle in the wind.
There is no time for comedy;
every stone regains hope and dies immediately.

Winter Pond

For Christophe de Menil

A tulip dives into the icy water to find a fish.
It swims in and out of the reflections
of the mountains.
It shows a kind of agitation that circulates
in the water.
The ripples move toward the forehead of the viewer.
The tulip goes swimming
not in search of the fish
but of the viewer's soul.
To the tulip the viewer's soul is flat like the
face of a child.
The soul prefers a small bed of ashes inside a whale.
The tulip has no memory.
The fish continue to watch the horizons of the earth
glide into the arctic flowers.

The Hand

The hand is all heart. It hops around like a toad to prove its dexterity. It presses your pockets on cold winter days and, in its profound state, polishes an apple for you. Silently it waits in the subways when it rains and is more of a hand than ever. It emerges from your humid coat, like a swollen hyena with its rancorous juices, to offer the young lady next to you a flat heart. Of course you get a slap and someone's boring hand dials the police, who arrive with fat hand . . .

The hand requires few words. It howls, repels odors and keeps the body of its lover from becoming slippery. A drop of water splashes in the crater of its palm, Merlin's pure lapis in the middle of the night. The lover's hand imagines itself a lover in the flabbiness of a perspiring torso, rolling in the wash of sighs. Armless, the hand spanks and slides around the mass of the sexual object with giant fingers that appear like rubber slugs in the moonlight.

My Heart

My heart is the shyest object in the world. It has numerous
qualities carelessly mixed together and insectlike roots that can
perceive the entire universe in an instant. It blushes when
it dies or becomes a monster when it loves. Imagine
the size of it when you undress. It becomes a periscope
each spring. It would like to be a lighthouse instead of being
in my chest. It is blind to joy and obligation, and in solitude,
threatens to burst. It is an expensive organ just inches
away from my mouth and thinks of itself as a praying mantis
or a phantom without a head. Gravity confuses it when I am
alarmed, and it would worship the sun on a stone.
When I sleep it is in a state of permanent repentance
and sinks to the bottom of my churning dreams.

On Poetry

Below me my feet are persistent, the marks on them
are whispers. Of course they do not respond to my obsessions.
My obsessions collapse in order to sacrifice themselves.
One might almost say I'm mad because I humble myself
before gravity. The table I write on is stubborn.
It defies gravity with its four legs and would sooner laugh at me.
The definition of obsession is a pathological anxiety,
fearsome, devious, that flirts with water. It is the exclusive
influence of poetry. The poet's instability makes him obedient
to a sheet of paper, and the slightest stir creates a small factory
like childbirth and human stupidity. Poetry is pinker
than nature, devastates every heart but owes itself nothing.
It does not require air and is not agile. The face of poetry
is an expressive cut of meat that gives us a glimpse of truth.

Poem from Amor

There are no bones in poverty and
pain.   You advise me to write poems of
insanity, poems of a face eternally hidden

by laughter.   Spain's greatest architect
slept with you a quarter
of a century ago.   Now I am your youngest poet, and

fill your bed with ink.   In the other world, in
other words, I threw away my shoes looking
for you on the throat of a

flower.   The eyes of the brolacchan lack
the great gentleness of paradise.   And I live in the vague
terror you will call and offer me a summer song and coffee.

The Future

There is
A white fish turning on its stomach
Pressing great things against my pants
Like an animal made of snow
It would be terrible if I were the sun
Melting her on everyone
Season after season
I am born a son
What if after
So much eternity
I outlived her?
My son would be the darkness
Between the seasons
The imitations of moonlight
No
He would be the fortune teller's mirror
In a coffee cup
The last hallucination of the hunted fox.

Maiz

The only bitter thing
About my father is
His dreams
Elegant ears of corn
The offertory of the earth
The fertility of rustic organs
And the iron lush of future ruins

Anger makes an afternoon a child
And the sorrow of the world a scar

Nine female clouds chant in anger
My father's death was a snowflake
In the river
His beard covered
The light poetry of the catafalque
As the insects of the world carried
Him to catch up with the day

FROM

Tulum

Tu Baño

Do you see my heart?
It can measure joy
it can see the
distance that causes
pain
it separates night
and day
it can demolish peace
and war
but
it grows
when you undress
it becomes a tiny
compass that follows
you into the shower
and it envies the grains
of water
and the swallows
that caress your
body
traveling
the white distance
seeking
the twilight
of the sea
and
its spacious life
its dark branches
of creation
and at that moment

my life is over
in a flash
of foam.

8.11.93

Siempre el Fuego

When I was young I could fly
wearing someone else's shoes

I would close my eyes
and find
your whole body in my open hand
or a cluster of memories in someone else's hair
gradually I would emerge
drunk and addicted

I was killed
and returned
to earth
with the stones
and the little flowers
the ones
with fire in their eyes

I see your figure cross the room
the figure I am committed to wound
without destroying myself
my life
like all life
that loves
your smell
the permanence of sleeping with you
the tale of the sheets
the gossip of the walls
is what makes this house
a man and a woman

every day
I am a
human being
because
all life is love
when the fire
arrives
with you
and
suddenly
I am alive
again
and
again.

Mi Tierra

Butterfly
Snow lips

When I touch you
I see Utah
your flat white sandy belly
the powdered dust devils in your navel
the white nipples of the Rocky Mountains
the color of corn and snow in your hair
and as my fingers follow the highways
down your back into the flat lands
where your waist meets the rivers
at the base of the grand canyon
I am carried south on your rushing waters
panning for gold
I discover your scattered kisses in the sand

Butterfly
Snow lips

This is
where sleep covers water
where our lips lie in wait
where stones are worn away
where fishermen gamble for our kisses
to tell us the secret of life
of your beauty upon this earth
of our love that burns the fire between us
giving life back to life

where I place my mouth
on this map
on this earth
on your
lips.

10.17.93

Tulum

Do you remember
the island we met
on our honeymoon

it wore a crown of gold
for you
when you walked
upon it
your feet lost their leaves
marking the sands forever
and the Mayan green waters
flourished when you
finally
stepped into my life

we occupied the hotel room
the one that waited for you
since last year
when we blessed it
with sand
with souvenirs
the ocean keeps
for us in its arms
until it grows old
watching us sleep

do you remember Arturo
who each year
greets us
with the keys to our room
and tells us
that the island is well

that the island will grow more flowers
because you will walk upon it
that the ocean will shed its frown
when it joins you
each morning for your swim
that the moon will appear tonight
to give you a drop of its blood
that all the new born stones
await your secret kiss
to build the wall of the world
to contain
my love
for you
my beloved
my love

This is our island
our coral
gleaming
with the naked things
I adore
in the mornings
where my tongue
lives
with your skin
in the happiest
house on earth

this slender strip of sand
with its ruins
devours our movements
on its beaches
it shall wait for us each November
as autumn departs in the north

seeking our island
our nights of sand
where the sky makes no sound
as it gathers our salt
to catch
our departing
kisses.

10.30.93

FROM

Orfeo/New Poems

The Skeletons

the skeleton of the butterfly
dreams of the boy who chases it

I think of you because
if I don't I'll disappear
like a thousand years
in a snake's eye

the rain wants to follow you to bed
it wants to glide with you in the shower
it wants to come inside our house
to watch my lips

love makes a wooden door
the key to the door is a fiery tongue
I hang my picture on the door

the icicle in the sky is wrong
I have a soul
it looks like a dirty window
the conquistadors left behind

my heart thinks
you are a mountain
with eyes
hiding our son
who sails into
manhood on our
skeletons

2.12.94

This Is a Poem About My Life

the grapes
remind me of the whales
gathering salt for the ocean

this is a poem about my life

you've interrupted
my life and death schedule
which gives me that poetic look each day

this is a poem about my life

where was I before I met you?
I was eroding on my way to work
and slept a lot
deep in the subways

this is a poem about my life

then I met your lips
on that windy day
I stopped poisoning my life
on Monday mornings

this is a poem about my life

when I met you
you were undressed
like a stone in the rain
I swam after utterly naked

this is a poem about my life

before you leave me to heal
I will find you someone to love
who will be shaped like a box

this is a poem about my life

before you leave me to heal
I will become an apple
and hide in a clock

this is a poem about my life

I will plant these wild lines
they will grow into honey
and weep in the spring
for you

2.14.94

March '94

I almost slept in my sleep
I almost had a dream
that the rain fell asleep
and dreamt of leaves and wind

it's good to be a dreamer
in March watching the snow comb
the city
watching the bundles move
on their way to work
the nuns tunneling the snow
trying to reach the children
before the light changes to red

the crabs spread salt on the eels
that move the buses
the gods of gloves and coats
watch the year fall to pieces

I'm dreaming of coats
of their secret women
of their children
hidden in their gloves

I have nothing on my mind
except the stillness of the queen
her winter hair
her glass heart
her white tears
become snow when
the sun breaks her heart

the stars are sailing in the sky
the statues are undressing with the clouds
as the snow leaves its history
on the city
all I feel is spring
as it collects its medals
and passes them on to us.

3.6.94

Children of the Fish

For Matt & Christophe

Do fish stare at the stars?
Do they take care of their children as well as I do?
Do they call their children every day?
Do they know where their children are?

I'm obsessed by my creations:

My son is a monster
who consumes money,
food, and music paper.

When my daughter looks at me,
my heart becomes an orphan
safe from the past and the future.

3.8.94

Easter

To David and Lindsey Shapiro

This is Easter:
The season of dead fish
and someone's dried blood
in a cup.

I want to preserve
the secret of the
shriveled leaves
Jesus Christ left
the locust
in his benevolence.

I want to preserve
the tiny clenched fist
of souls tying their
shoes with benedictions
as they drift down
in prayer.

Will I come to rest
in one of God's hands?

The one that holds
Manson and Hitler?

Did the angels ever
visit Auschwitz?

So,
why can't I speak

to God frankly and
discuss the mysteries
of my life?

Each leaf
is a human face
falling to earth.

For a moment
I almost believed
one of them was mine.

3.26.94

Palm Sunday

Babies are born
in the subways
on Palm Sunday.

They can neither see
nor hear because their
parents are at church
gathering grass for
their collective sins.

Sins are creatures
with academic thoughts:
The Gestapo understood
sin as being intelligent
and misunderstood
and,
perhaps,
even noble.

They protected
their sins
from the blazing sun
and guarded them gently
from the eyes of
ingenuous justice.

They only questioned
the flesh
as sin has no spirit
or soul
to speak of
and would pass them

through the fire
in seconds.

On Palm Sunday
we celebrate
the beginning
and the end of

one Jew
with dead grass,
hand shakes and smiles
to end all the sins
of the world.

3.27.94

Tattoo

I have a picture of you
tattooed on the palm of my hand.

I keep that hand on my lap
on my way to work in the subway,
and often wonder if anyone
notices that I'm staring at you,
because I remember sleeping
with you in my hand
the night before.

My other hand has an eye
that stares at you
when I take a shower.
The hand with your picture
likes to scratch my head
because you once said
you liked my hair.

When my hand,
the one with the eye,
answers the phone
when you call,
it blinks
and is overjoyed
to hear your voice
because your picture
cannot talk to it
when I rub both
my hands together.

And if I were to die
without seeing you again,
if I were to die before
I could spend the rest
of my life with you,
the hand with the eye
would lie across my chest
upon my heart
and the one with your picture
would cover my eyes
and both would dream
of you.

3.29.94

Lost Things

You are wrong.

The snow lives in the sky
with an angel
who hides God in a storm.

I was bitten and torn apart
before you were born.

The nude I used to follow to work
has given me flowers
and wants to take me out to lunch.

You see,
I'm not alone in the dark.

I'm in the arms of hope.

4.5.94

The Cedar

To Mike and Lynn

The shadow of the twentieth century
lives on in my liver with all the dead poets
and artists who drank at the Cedar Bar.

Who said they died for chamber music
and blanquette de veau?
Who said they found one another pounding
glasses of booze against the broken afternoon?

Every night they talked of art and ate museums.
They were the bones of whiskey and the gods of color.
They frightened space with their eyes and apologized to their
brushes because the world could not see them paint.

The critics were stars imitating Rome.
The artists were silent and became New York.

They treated love like relics in a bed
And gave life away for free.
Their hearts bled fresh blood
becoming accidents on white streets
that would hang in museums.

When they spoke about life,
their words became waves of suicide.
Proof that life imitates life.

4.6.94

Orfeo

To my friends

Each hair is a poem I gave my son
Each hair is my allowance from the universe
Each hair is a sunspot on someone's broken heart

The secrets that emerge from the psyche have no floor
They will get off on any floor when you least expect them to
They wear shadows that look like my mother
She could stop God but could not make it snow
She said the weather was a work of art
Like the last streak of wonder
In Medea's heart

You don't have to watch human
Sacrifice on television
Shut your window
Lock the door
Wait for yourself
In the corner
In the night
In the little house
That holds your tears

There is no piano
Just your green velvet
And the years you spent in Russia
As a little box in your mother's womb
With all her curses and her dreams of men

When I write poetry I hear voices:
KennethKoch rubbing his forehead

DavidShapiro swatting words
FrankOHara blowing his noise
PhilipBryant smiling upon me
Neruda drinking red wine
Lorca hailing a cab in NewYork
Vallejo walking in Paris
RonPadgett calming the world
TedBerrigan dignifying wise-guy poetry
JoeCeravolo on the radio with
Melanoma in the milky sky
Are you asleep?
No
Chopin is asleep on our new sofa
He is wasting his life away
His health looks like a dirty window
His heart has a broken leg
His breathing will go to the grave with him

I'm not one to part
I'm not one to hide my feelings
I'm the end of the corridor in your hands
This is a song of war
Because love is music
And its ferocious notes
Are oars that pull us apart

Death is incredible
It is man made
We change the names of the dead
When we bury them
In time they look back at us
And see us
The living
Like old doors in the wind

In the beginning there were small islands
Floating on poetry
These islands belonged to Joe Ceravolo
Joe's words are the body parts of poetry
Like the little children of the fireflies
Who set songs on fire when we cry

There is work to do on top of the forest
There are too many words on top of the forest
They are obscuring our conversation
If the trees aren't pruned our words will never reach
Their destination:
The telephones that hate love
And protect the dead from the living

Will my daughter dress like Venus
Wrapped in exaggerated hopes?
Will the pill invent love for her?
Will her life take place on a
Mental and spiritual planet?
Yes
No
My daughter is a seed full of steam
Leaving me behind like a bad marriage
Helen Helen
My Helen of Troy
Once I placed a kiss on a spider's web
Because there is no evil in nature
The spider laughed
Now the kiss is as free as an insect
And the better part of our love

My other marriages were like the four seasons
That come and go

They have left me small stones
That spend their nights on the balcony of life
Watching Pathos and Comedy celebrate their wedding

Tonight I will write poetry
I will pile the world on my pillow
Like a paramilitary sous chef
Toss an avalanche of flowers
With sunlight and olive oil.

(David Shapiro)

4.25.94

Culo Prieto

Naranjito / Puerto Rico

I do not know what afternoon I will die
I do not know when in the afternoon I will die

The years are not my brother
They have become lullabies of harm
And the fallen trees of my youth

My grandfather told me the palm tree
Was the strongest tree on the island
It could withstand the roof of music
And the pounding shoes of the rain

He told me these things
As he ate running cheese
That hard work was not good for the soul
That the soul needed food and expensive drink
That the end of life was as flat as the world

His life was the introduction to forgiveness
He had the heart of a dam
He was the refill of humor
And to my grandmother
He was the slave of the moon

She was a rare bullet in his heart
That he fondled at night
And like a cloud of decoys
He said to her

O my tropical infamy
you are the top of the rain
hunger is fake happiness without you
do not die
I will run for you

9.15.94

Joe Ceravolo

Divorce fertilizer
        apache air fare
Are the power of the rock
The young swim for the enemy
And reach the beach of lions
They are all the stars of the woods
Ah felony felony
You are the chocolate of the wolf!
I am the son of lilac
The funnel of corn
Antarctica is the last poet
Not the amputee in the subway
Milk sunsets why is god a harpoon?
May the hand of train bless him
Love is full of noisy names
Coffee shops and soft Pliocene poetry
Like   eros and voiceless sex
Offering   water
        innocent peninsula
Like a   Sunday and jello kisses
Nothing less than summer id
O music Helen
Sleeping dollar bill
Aluminum pleasure
Elevator meat
The yellow hook of Pan
        offering
        the meadow of souls
Yes! Yes!
This is my blood
This is my poem.

10.19.94

Whispers

To my son

May the whispers and cantatas from heaven join
you in your life like the inches in art

May Kenneth's spirit always dwell in your green
syntax

May the well of David's poetry touch your writing
hand

May the anomalous spirit of Mozart keep a glove in
your heart

May the blue beaches of music always embrace you
when you arrive with your poetic snowman

May you always be a flying star pushing the beginning
of creation to the open door

May the memory of birds swim blindly in your
heart like astronauts in cold outer space

May the conquistador's ivory blood and the roses
in Montezuma's skull stitch your life together

And may the crayon hands and snakes swim with me
and my father who is a cave full of gifts from you.

4.15.95

Oklahoma America

       The fathers of America
have ruined the mountains
       The mothers of America
have dried the river beds
       The children of America
are dying at play
       Our forefathers watch our
neonates mouse the words of freedom
       Worms vagrant fallopian worms

Are birds freedom?
Are children sheep?

This is the year of the bullet
Of white professional homework
Of Nagasaki fertilizer
Of cheap fuel oil
Of tender SS movies
This is oncotic Americana
This is why fish will fly to heaven

We are the widow of our dreams
We are shrinking in their skin
We are attached to their wisdom

Look at the thermos colored sky
Fame flying on TV
They wash their hands in our womb
Where the dead know the stars
Are sleeping children
Like the procession of the equinox
Condensing our fate

We are the Furies of entropy
We have killed
A hundred sixty million
Human trees this century

Who will wear their clothes?
Death is as round as an apple
Holding a child ever so gently

They no longer see the kangaroo
They cannot touch
The innocent mirror
With their wet hands
The tears are drowning
In their sand pails
Like lyrical lips
The mothers will never be
The sun on their faces

O my beloved country
Where is the antelope of love?
Why does the earth
Turn away from the sun?
Why are the children covered
With concrete
Rain
And neglected
Specks of freedom?

4.25.95

FROM

The Beatitudes

(1997–2000)

A Brief History of Genesis

Introduction

I am writing this deposition using the seven pages
Allotted to describe primitive dispositions to be submitted for
Review of the evolutionary events that occurred during my
Observations of the creation of the human book of Genesis.

I have eaten one of the humans in real time in the
Interest of our superior science and because I was terribly
Hungry and dispirited by their arrogant actions. Having done
This, the following narrative followed:

Day One

These carbon-based life forms transude large emotions that
Resemble payphones. Their central star warms the humming
In their ears when they procreate. Like an open mouth,
They dream of space travel. They think of us as the
Yellow eyes of Seeing Eye dogs. They have subdivided
Themselves into two species they have named human man
And human woman. The woman wears a large dorsal fin
To negotiate an aqueous truth in a receptacle they call *love*.
After copulation the mated pair nail themselves to each other
And begin the termination of their legal bond.

Day Two

We have been the subject of much discussion throughout
Their history. They have described us as the beginning of
Some mysterious legend: A legend with a superior brain and
Extraordinary large haunting eyes. The body fluids of these
Creepy-crawly bipeds organize into puddles. These puddles

Become trances, thumbnails, the toe of some supernatural
Being, or a splinter in the soul of someone they wish to
Influence.

Day Three

To study these occupiers, defecators of all natural and
Beautiful things, and to fully comprehend their atrocious
Actions, we should become human life-forms; buy a business
To maximize our observations pretending to be a boy's father
Who is a winner. We could also become the screaming hand
Over a woman's mouth. Isn't that what this extremity is for?
We would feel their immediate truth of true punishment.

Day Four

Their belief system is an emblem made of wood, or a human
The color of a yellow flower in a desert. This chthonian deity
Neither nourished itself nor drank fluids in the desert. The
Camel is never mentioned in any of its voluminous, devotional
Writings. This is the gaping hole in the human condition.
Why do they want to pierce the sky with needles? Do they
Think they can bleed the sky like a star? They do not know
The standing oceans on their planet *are* the skies. The
Chemicals on their hairy corporal forms are actually moist
Radiation.

Day Five

The small neurotic ventriloquist in the chest cavity lies to
Them all their lives. It controls the light between their bodies
In the darkness, when they squeeze themselves against each

Other. Squeals emanate from this particular foot-stomping
Organ that controls the actions of the most improbable
Positions.

Day Six

It would appear they communicate to each other by random
Impulses. These sounds are the production of the crowded,
Disorganized warehouse at the opposite end of the gravity that
Divides the biped's body. On this flat surface, the sounds
Symbolize a language and, perhaps, a thought process
Indicating intelligence. Or, are they regurgitating? They
Conjure time to celebrate space travel. Although they have
Never ventured beyond their star system.

Day Seven

Their common belief system is a blue light that blinked out at
Some point in time in their short history. This history is brief
When compared to the open windows of the stars. This
Light, scintillating from a piece of broken glass they
Themselves attacked and shattered, is even beyond logic. Why
These creatures worship a light source that they cannot
Scientifically prove, that there is no physical evidence thereof,
But many witnesses, is even beyond *their* comprehension.
What is more baffling, is that these humans, as they call
Themselves, endeavor throughout their lives to become the
Autochthonous cracks in this enameled legend.

3.1.98

Eternity

in the beginning
there was no end

the ground we
walked on was
a memory

our shadows
false stories

our clothing
space without time

darkness was the
color of angels

and the stars did
not weep

2.25.98

New Testament to Sadness

I watched the restless tongue of God
        in the Providence of his closet
create impulsive limbs and
        emblazon dreams
that I would wear as heaven's bondage
        until the end of forgiveness

I owe my sadness to fallen leaves
I owe my sadness to oceans of small breasts
I owe my sadness to the smile of strawberries
I owe my sadness to a child's heart beating like a frightened bird
I owe my sadness to my Father's dusty sadness
I owe my sadness to my clean socks
I owe my sadness to the painted trees
I owe my sadness to things as warm as bread

7.9.98

FROM

Incidents of Travel in Poetry

(1997–2002)

Incidents of Travel in Poetry

Happy Birthday Kenneth Koch / Feb 27

We went to all those places where they restore sadness and joy
and call it art. We were piloted by Auden who became
Unbearably acrimonious when we dropped off Senghor into the
steamy skies of his beloved West Africa. The termites and ants
were waiting for him to unearth the sun in Elissa. The clouds
were as cool as a dog's nose pressed against our cheeks. I
notice your eggshell skin is as creamy as a lion's armpit as we
cross the horizon on strands of Yeats' silver hair. There is a
light coffee flame in his eyes guiding us like an old Irish house
cleaner holding a candle in a black and white English movie.
Yeats' lips look like an angry Rimbaud illuminating poetry with
his youth and vigorous sunlight. He knew eternity would vanish
the sun at dusk. He caught it with a rainbow tied to his finger.
There was nothing left after that. We cross the equator
heading north following Emily Dickinson's black bag containing
stems of her longer poems preserved in darkness and memory
like wild pearls thrown overboard to avoid capture by Spanish
pirates. The islands below float by like water hearts in a child's
aquarium. We are candy wrappers being blown across the
waxed floors of poetry. We land on the Brooklyn Bridge.
Whitman's past-port face is grinning at the nineteenth century
in the thorny arms of Gerard Manley Hopkins whose head was
set on fire by God's little hands. The hands that circumcised
the world. Gertrude Stein is a match flaring on a young
woman's pillow whose birthmarks have been stolen. We cross
the green Atlantic into World War One. We are met by Rilke
dressed in his Orpheus uniform wearing white sonnet gloves
that once belonged to a stone angel. Rilke offers us a glass of
amontillado made from Lorca's private stock of gypsy tears.
The sherry is not quite as dry as Wallace Stevens' lush mango

metaphors of familiar objects. Although Stevens' poems are fragrant, there is a lingering afterthought of Pound on the tongue. Pound collected his misty feelings to make raindrops into European and American poetry. Vagueness became as sharp as a pencil. Our blue box is not allowed to attend Apollinaire's birthday party held by the august *Académie française* on the Eiffel Tower. He is being awarded the "Golden Frog Souffle Award" and a one-way ticket to the Greek and Roman past to spend afternoons with Williams filling wheel barrows with the twentieth century. Both Apollinaire and Williams could hail a cab on Madison Avenue in any country. After the bash we toured Paris and London with D.H. Lawrence who kept stopping to relieve himself of the great mysteries of life whenever we went by a Bavarian gentian plant. He claimed he was writing poetry for his new book: Acts of Attention for Love Poems. Eliot was rebuilding London when we left. It reminded him of Detroit or Cincinnati or Saint Louis. He was removing despair from the weather. He thought it affected people's minds and did not want to overload Mayakovsky's emptiness with old English churches that pray for water heaters and cloudless nights. Mayakovsky, on the other hand, insisted there were bugs in Russia who could write poetry just as interestingly as Eliot. The Russian winter is elegant cruelty compared with the English milk-toast weather: "A man without a cloud in his trousers is not a man." Eliot thought this was the most boring statement he had ever heard. Although Cummings' poems appear unintentional on the surface, he did not act like a drunken amputee at the dinner table and always said pleasant things that came out of nowhere. His conversation was experimental but logical and he investigated words, mixing them on paper with a pencil. Cummings was all *etcetera* after a few drinks. We move the sun to South America. Neruda had become an organic poet writing about the fulcra of *yes* and *no*. He wasn't home when we got there, so we went over to Allen's for some microbiotic poetry. As usual, Allen was rolling incense and howling at America. Allen was always mystical and beautiful when he walked on the Lower East Side. When he stepped into the old Jewish pavement, he mystified the habitués. David Shapiro, the Djinn of subatomic poetry, asked Allen what was the future of poetry in the borough of Queens? Allen placed the palm of his right hand on David's glistening forehead and said: "David, don't you know? The future has no future. It is very old and doesn't worry about its future anymore, because it has so little left of it." Allen made suicide exhilarating when he wrote Kaddish. Finally, suicide could talk about the pain of living with unbearable beauty. Beauty was Frank O'Hara talking to Second Avenue with a diamond in his head. We were the personal details in Frank's harem of private lives when LeRoi insisted on becoming black, abandoning us for a noble cause, according to Frank, who loved Imamu Amiri Baraka. We were the details in Frank's poems and living one's life was a detail in Frank's life. John Ashbery arrived from Paris on a plane made of expensive suits, shirts and ties. Like his poems, he was sparkling and squeaky clean, dressed in elegant language. He is the daydream that had become a poet. His subject is to have no subject. Perhaps a casual reference to someone special. He is a poet of the less obvious in life: the sestina made of clouds. We crossed the equator on our way to a cocktail party for Gary Snyder. There is no other life for his outdoor poems, hitchhiking on hands-on love. Gary seems to have time to write poems about the notes in his life. Kenneth, on the other hand, has a paper cup full of wonderful poems. He can write a poem about a cathedral living in a paper cup. Kenneth travels everywhere with his paper cup. At a certain time of day, Kenneth finds room in his paper cup for perfect days and perfect moments:

Perfect moments when Frank spoke to us.
Perfect moments when Allen spoke to us.
And they sang to us
with human wings
upon which we sleep.

10.7.97

Christophe Lima

Today the sun came out to greet
The People's Republic of Flushing.
And
I'm going to take my daughter to the movies.
She is cinnamon and Italian like her mother's temper.
She is brilliant blue like her mother's eyes.
She is a brimming water glass of iridescent
Ideas about how I should grow up.

A short walk paddling the sky toward the movie,
With the wind and the sun along Northern Boulevard.
We're looking forward to popcorn,
With trace elements of fun.

We'll stop by "Puff & Smoke" and pick up
Some 50/50 glycol fluid for my cloudless cigars.
We'll have that "unwarranted talk" that divorced fathers
Have with a teenage daughter.
We'll peel away her mother's deciduous
"Visitation Rights."

"This is the colorful democracy of divorce,
With its custodial incidence of children."

I remember her face floating in her mother's arms:
A lightly powdered football wrapped in pink.
She is the ice and molten water that run across my life,
Burning the tears in the palm of my hand.

My daughter is a teenage vegetarian,
Who will not eat meatloaf.

Because bovines are herbivores ruminating
On sheets of grass dusted by atomic rain.

I notice the lipstick she's wearing,
Like a troubled heart,
Looking for mindless love,
And the quality of adult life,
Forgotten by the seeds of the dead.

I look up from our walk to notice the weather:
The clouds are tinted with catholic grey,
Violet repentance and prudent parental support.
Each word she speaks to me is a rarity.
Of pre-Colombian pottery living on borrowed time.

After the movie *Space Jam*
(black & white giraffes playing basketball with Bugs Bunny),
I walk her home to her mother's fenestrations,
And tell her:

> Of my inflamed liver,
> Raging at me for covering
> It with cirrhosis,
> Bourbon and beer.
> She's afraid my liver will set
> The world on fire while I'm driving.

She asks me if I'm going to die and I tell her:
I will always be there for her,
Like the clean faces in an old photograph.

At home she shows me the bruises
She suffered at her last hockey game.

Her new stick is curved at the end,
Like the canthus of a tiger's eye.

She hugs me as if I were a giant pyramid.
I think of the repetitive memory I'll leave her,
All wrapped up in myself,
Exposing my side road of self-esteem,
And its harsh light of poetry
—unrelenting and grinding—
With its unexpected bits of sunshine.

11.24.96

Michael Gizzi's Famous Liver

Mice are pouring out of your pockets every time you move
You strap yourself into a chair
They know how old and pale you are
Counting your leftover love letters
One love letter picks another "I loved you last"
The doctors are as vague as the squiggly
Riddles on your medical chart
You recognize the bony face of your last poem
You resuscitate it six times a day
It will be the poem's last life
The poem's eyes follow you
Watching every move you make on the page
This poem is not your last stop
And when you write Allah glows in the desert
Because you are special
Because the hairs in your ear are long
Because the hairs on your nose are long
And the top of your head is the largest
And least cluttered place on your body
Your wife or your lover is not a prune
That doesn't close the bathroom door
Privacy is no longer the secret of love
You are the great poet from another dream
As the night nurse steps out
Who looks like long ago
And someone else
And turns you over
For your evening walk

Epicedium to Potter's Field

My father was
A blossom,
And I was his fragile
Epiphyte on his
Days off.
The purple
Dogs of years
Gone by
Watch him smile
At the horizon.
His feretory
Catches the
Rain from the
Smoldering sky.
These fields are
Fallow and dried
Gullies where gin
Sparkled
In the morning.
My father's remains
Are smooth like the
Starlight that
Makes my life
Slightly yellow.

2.24.97

Ode to Vanessa del Rio

I'm unconscious again. Who will bring back me this time?
Will it be the dream or the double agents, Cleopatra, Helen of Troy,
Marilyn Monroe or Vanessa del Rio? The air is all octaves when they
Lick their way through my head. My solos receive honors as I sort
Through the vacant lots of tenderness. I would trade my terror
To have had my heart broken by any one of them. So I have said
Often in a fit of sorcery. Any organ is home or a wheatfield of color

When they smiled. Like ghosts, they sweat the most secret things
That swim. The photocopier makes the stars seem nearer,
Like gift-wrapped lilacs in the dark. Overhead the distributor of allegories
And sunbathers is looking for an old photo of the
Blameless star that crushed the last discarded matter of innocence.
This is the winter nurse dispensing babble as we boil down our old
Reveries. This reduction gives us a new understanding of our

Fading memories. Something passes us by, but we continue to drive
On like bubbles blissfully taking our tears wherever they wish to go.
My last fax had no memory, no gender to speak of, and thought touch
And affection were as inconvenient as the renaissance is to modern
Science. In another hospital, the grandiose illness is strolling across
What is left of daylight. It is looking for the golden shepherdess who
Gathers our voices into a small lake that writes romantic poetry on a

Cold contemporary machine. The truest falsehood is human thought:
The sweet myth and hollow shell that gave birth to Romeo and Juliet.
I look at you, see forever and how foolish I am pretending to be a
Stammering frog you kissed on a kid's TV show. Someday my son will
Lose consciousness as I did, when he meets the woman who dreamt of
Me. Meanwhile, I'll continue watching TV, eating my TV dinners
With plastic silver forks hoping to become a frog again.

Scene Two (In the Fog)

For Joseph Lease

I'm exhausted and lovesick with my own fancy sickness.
The art of cruelty with its temples cannot move
When all the leaves in the world are at the bottom

Of the pool. And what is all this talk of men whose lives
Are trees hanging delirious puppets in their minds?
In this paradise of personal hatred, hope is a boat made

Of primitive wishes. I have never regretted choosing
The immense riddle which sees me as I truly am,
Sometimes offering joy to someone on a bus. I should have

Been a poet like the sparks of morning light on some mountains.
Also thin rain stretched across someone's lips who glanced
At me on my way to work. These events are the worn slippers

Of our tragic history. But I was the sound of old men laughing at
Empty paint cans between their legs that gave me the time of day.
Their smiles are a warm day in autumn. The past in their eyes

Betrays their disappointments and untrustworthy secrets.
These actors lost their manuals on the uses of life,
Expecting they'd find the truth about dying tomorrow.

2.27.00

Bittersweet

Can you see them in the wind? My telephone calls you.
Are you strong enough to listen?
This wind has a fief of its own and wants to share it with you
In one of the chambers of your ear. It wants to know which side of

Your face to cool when you are stressed,
Where to take you when you dream,
To dry you after you shower.
The wind is blind, it has no notion about what you look like,

Yet it can feel your voice when you speak. It is tacitly limited but can smell
The scenery of your classic skin. It likes both sides of your body,
Especially when you sleep on your stomach. Although the wind is reticent
With secrets and enjoys the games of the soul, it dreams of paradise in

Your lungs, of the erotic recesses in the tropics.
When the wind travels on portraits of the ocean,
The globe turns its face to be caressed and sees you and the games of an
Old man fishing for the past leaving his mind and body to be with you in

An orderly way. You are the breeze that continues to turn the pages of
My life. A pinch of forgetfulness could be worse than death itself.
The breeze carries wishes in a bird cage the shape of a breathing
Nostalgia. I go on consulting the vacancies in my life, that I have leased

For money, to collect the past for meaningful moments of wisdom to
Repeat themselves to include us again in a portion inside time that would
Fit us as we were, when ferns were the only things to eat. Love is always
Mysteriously present, even when the world ended the first time in the

Tributaries of naïveté. We were to save it from itself. Why should the
Stars and their beautiful suburbs be interested in us as the expansion of
Love, knowing our hearts are small and permanent anomalies? This easel
Upon which our dreams are of painted daylight, is the secret

Of our times in the lapses of happiness. Nevertheless, we arrived
Late to enjoy the buffet of witnesses. No previous life was like this, there
Was no breeze to touch, to cool us after a vigorous discussion about the
Lapidary cosmos, its house of Tarot cards. This was a figment of the

Waterwheel of imagined moments that we pursue when reminded
We are totally to ourselves in the end. Nevertheless, the previous
Lives are haunting, remanding us with promises of leisure "poetic" times
And warm corridors of youth.

Can we live here again before it closes to public sentiment?
How wonderful it is to fly into previous days to rest, take stock of our
Wounds of bittersweet memories. Still, life is a little early today
And my lapses are waiting for you.

3.10.02

Guadalajara City

For Francisco Pellizzi

Both gravity and love keep me from flying off the earth
And force me to awake in Guadalajara City which is the color
Of roses that die in my mouth every time I leave. North of
Here is the grey life of winter with its insistence on the equality
Of cold weather. Obviously I'm in love with

Mexico, with its green and red wings, with its shy snakes
That whisper to the young tourist girls, admonishing them
With their creamy blue and yellow fans heating their dreams.
All of a sudden the girls realize their hearts are lakes where the
Boys swim nude like brown autumn leaves on rushing

White water. The music is always louder here and the
Cloudy bottles of booze breathe better when you buy them.
They don't want to be abandoned on a dusty shelf
With a bunch of cockroaches intoxicated with AA. So I
Cancel my life and settle for the sun's consolation prize

Back to my childhood, to the beginning of footsteps that are the
Last to know when you are gone. If you decide to come
With me to Guadalajara to visit the housetops with their
Lemon and pink marzipan crucifixes, it's important you bring
My father's reflection without its bitterness and let me walk

In your sleep, because my need to think of you is stronger
Than bitterness. Tequila is as clear as a shooting star
And as vernal as a New York menu demanding snails
Pneumonia and birds salmonella under glass. No one cares
If you forget me immediately when you arrive in this city of

Large hearts that sleep unarmed with the dead.
They wash our bubble to enter it as we enter each other's
Crazy emotions, because our hearts live in the foam of their
Own drama. Our Lady of Guadalupe will take us out for
Arabic coffee and horseback riding on Spanish horses.
We'll drink water from hidden cisterns in clear glasses made

Of churches. We'll get drunk on chocolate as we did
Discovering for the first time the erotic apprehension of
Our touch. There is only you in the steps of my life,
And I need you like the immortal smile of a monocle.
If we die here, blowing the clouds away with clean

Handkerchiefs, Mexico will be the Paris we spent wisely
In our youth. It's true we cannot escape the smoke that
Follows the wreckage of our souls. Nevertheless we're
Portraits of that smoke, of its prayers of childhood,
Of its unexpected silence after making life in the sand.

1.20.00

Necromancy

I am always out of breath when I think. I walk endless miles in my sleep,
Along a beach people speak of when they are older and are no longer in
The throes of life's vexatious conclusions. It is difficult to see the evening
On this beach where each grain of sand represents a human hope,

And indifference. But everything is enchanted here, even the fugitive
Pirates buried here. Will my shadow function as well without me?
Or will it be relieved of my nonsense and thoughts of you?
There is no proof except the music will be beautiful and divine as I rock

Your foot to sleep. I was presented a wish, dripping with the vivid future,
A drug that would take effect on sunny beaches of mixed
Feelings where it is comfortable to be in doubt with one's opinions of life's
Acidulous ends. When I am rested, I will see you in slow motion as

You perform your routine as a gladiator clad in iron, like fixed opinions
On an elementary school blackboard. This is a time to contemplate things
Falling to and leaving earth. We are free to travel anywhere we wish,
To forget any one in our lives that would not rest with us.

There is no sleep in this unencumbered moment, only the recollections of
What you thought were divine, heavenly voices. You open your eyes for
What seems to be the last time. You enter the room, happy and glad to
Be alive. And notice you are admiringly happy to be here,

Like the tales of children who said we would. We become intoxicated
When we are told we can touch each other,
And say and take back all those things foolishly said. We are infinitely
Happy that at last we are the fluids between the stars.

8.12.01

A Layer of the Heart

I would take off my underwear and imagine I was an imploding star
Looking for a beam of light,
So I would not disappear in the demeaning darkness of space.
What would happen to the black sky of midnight without the stars?
A sparrow eaten by a cat.

I did not think my life would be like this. Perhaps I thought I would be
Traffic in some Italian opera directing rituals and spells cast on homeless
Lovers by the gods. I never thought I would meet someone like you.
Why should you care about the silver ants in my head that keep me up,
Sometimes all night making noise while they draw sketches of you?

And you. Your Greek stories are so different from mine, yours are
Covered with feta from the winter islands the gods could not
Take away from you. When I was about twelve years old or so,
I would imagine I would meet someone like you under the covers,
Especially when it was bitter cold outside.

12.11.01

À la Carte

Consommé and ice cream
—like eating clouds—
Are the legends of Western civilization
I believe in the myths
Of pineapples
Avocado vanilla and papaya
The Spaniards brought olive oil
To its knees and red wine
To the rainforest
Holding warm melons in their lascivious hands
Spitting out the naked pits into the breasted wind

Chefs
Nowadays
Kiss themselves up in the morning
When they make a mistake
It's no longer nouvelle cuisine
It's "American fusion cuisine"
On oversized plates that scintillate cold light
From brightly colored tiny toy foods
After an ambiguous confection
With an archaic espresso
That will androgynously swell
Your Diner's Club card
We leave a tip because it's
God's birthday and watch
The waiter go into "fugue"

AND!
You realize you've eaten a dead sunflower
And that all your friends are old poets
And that Joe Ceravolo is the bread and water
Of a charred soldier

Keats is an alcoholic beverage
And David Shapiro is a diamond being torn
Asunder by art and poetry
Rabbits are sexual organs
And Shakespeare was a screenwriter
As blind as a lightbulb
And we're really afraid of death
And being buried in a cereal box.

9.29.96

Environs of Saint Petersburg/Nov. '95

For Seth Rogovoy

From Frankfurt's clear stainless steel air

(we found no roaming Swastikas
just blond and green uniformed poster soldiers
bearing polite Mattel submachine guns)

we fly to the icy "Venice of the North"
following Pushkin in the clouds
to the environs of Saint Petersburg

It's November in Leningrad
(it's always November in Leningrad)
when Helen and I arrive
Stalin is not there to meet us

The KGB does not interrupt
our sleeping luggage
I want to appear as ordinary
as *smetana* on borsch
as we go through customs
our guide is waiting

She's a miniature "White Russian" Cossack
In a cranky Mercedes Benz
"I speak English" (with a Boston accent)
"My fiancé is Jewish"

Our imprints in the Russian snow
are as red as Pasternak's winter scarf
His shadow joins us for dinner that evening

At the hotel we are a new American city
lost between yesterday and Europe

How beautiful you must have been
during the "White Nights" of June
between the boars and drawbridges
where river Neva waited
a thousand years for Peter the Great

These fairy tales of Voltaire's Russia
are made of honey and Champagne
and as crowded as busy sunspots
as we cross *Nevsky Prospekt*
as wide as the Grand Canyon
on our way to the The Catherine Palace
Everyone is selling *Malassol/Osetra* caviar
in round tins we are told not to buy
especially in front of the stalagmite churches
piercing the sky like cocktail forks
in search of onions between the stars

Christ never shaved
for the resurrection of Russia
He is an icon of flat discolored driftwood
with the eyes of a startled doe
suffering the pain of smoky prayers

"The Grand Hotel Europe" is an antique samovar
with silver and glass elevators bobbing up and down
like Christmas lights on the Caspian Sea
The bathrooms are made of candy and European perfume

Every evening snow falls like a light madrigal
from the gulf of Finland, the thread of life in winter
on its way to the blue and yellow Hermitage

Among the anthracite ivory
and wrinkled leaves of gold
porous sugar rooms
are occupied with crystal
and startled marbled statues
stunned clouds captured
by the luminous hands of old masters
to become the daily bread of Catherine the Great
ruminating on dazzling cold Peter Carl Fabergé eggs for breakfast

These puffs of historic art
are guarded by old women
who have walked too many *versts*
in faded print dresses
surrounded by snow
as they wait for the kulaks to return
You quickly realize
this is their kitchen
and these are effects
of the "good Tsar"
(not the Hermitage not the "people")

"On the Russian Front" the scattered sap
of the "Germany Army" is incarcerated
in the trees that fell
in the blue tschernosem of the "Russian Soul"

We return to the fabled skies of home
with a few mica tears in our bags
noble and ugly.

10.28.96

Urbane Parables

A "Latino" parable:
What does leprosy mean
To a New York poet?
Herpes on parade.

1.
The prisoner of humanity writes poetry
About the last fictional hand closing
His eyes in a dream.

2.
In the dream a pizza is on the corner
Waiting for a prostitute that resembles
An antique pancake who will teach it
All about the "experience" of age
And how to make noises in the dark.

3.
So, your pet housefly, Keats,
Wants a chocolate envelope for Valentine's
Day; but can't decide how big it should be.
Bigger than Tony Towle's housefly, Milton,
At the very least.

4.
You receive a brown box in the mail with what's
Left of your liver, coated with the evaporated
Proverb: "Welcome the God of peace."

5.
"Henri" James shows up with a license to
Practice the empyrean "complexities of life."

He has become the natural adhesive of complex
American writing; the erotic anthem of nostalgic
English professors genuflecting, nude, on scattered,
Uncooked grains of rice.

6.
There is a poetic life in America, ask Helen Vendler.
Just pay your electrical bill. Speak English.
Remember, Mr. Hernando Cortez, *El Caudillo*,
Didn't speak English. Look what happened to him:
He left Spanish Harlem and wound up in the South Bronx;
The first "identificate MexicanPuertoRican" on methadone
With a liability of possible euphoria.

2.2.97

Dream

I went to Spain nude
Flying on a thin grey stone
It was in a dream
I remembered this morning
I went there to learn
To make wine old wine
Ancient wine ancient sails
Ancient buildings
Blue sherry and green port wine
An elderly woman
Took me by the hand
Toured me
In this dream
In a tiny town
With hot brick buildings
Yellow streets
In short white sleeves
Her soul was a neat
Handkerchief folded in her bag
She smiled and nodded
She told me she was once
Venus in lucent blue
Wearing French ice cream
And silver jeans when she
Whipped the colophon
On the clouds of poetry
Bringing epochal refinement
To Lorca
To Neruda
And quiet silence
Into the world

1.18.97

Poets

In the country
Of flowers, the poets
Are poisonous
They live in bars
And fish all day for poems
Yet they are the
Passionate tractors
That beat melodies
Into pine needles.
They have not
Forgotten the old cars
With poets in the back
Seat, the last of their
Kind, clutching poems
Written on memories
That undress them
At night and
Put them to bed.

2.25.97

The Weather

After Kenneth Koch

Snowflakes are human snowflakes
Snowflakes the size of a woman
Snowflakes that speak with a pink accent
Snowflakes with big salty eyes
Bluer than lightning half asleep
With centuries of poems exuviating
Othello's needy Desdemona
—I've lost my place—
No it's Sunday and I'm up early
Looking for my place
In that puff of light
Where heart is real
And as bright
As the invisible air
And as unsymbolic and grey
As Thomas Aquinas kissing someone
Could he have signed a document
"my lobe my lover our love"?
…don't think so
Just thoughts on life and benign results
On ocean liners of hugs and roses!
Tumbling with touch and life
And love with or without genital contact
(so firmly founded in counterpoint)
With or without "fragrance free"
Why refer to life
As scars and days as bars
And time (Rococo & Romantic) as pain?

Why write?
Since the highest enjoyment is a kiss
As endless as a rubber band

1.12.97

Luis Borges

The drizzle turned slowly into a quiet man
Who wants to save a nation
And its people from having their throats cut

For reading poetry
For writing poetry

The emperor of poetry accuses poetry of
Being the biggest lie in the known universe
Poets are accused of creating death at
The end of the world

For creating animals and landscapes
For creating themselves and other people
For creating bread and knives
For creating love in the middle of the night

Inside the secret walls of advancement
Where snow never melts
The remains of poetry are difficult to see
They are as invisible as conscience

These fragments are the imprisoned guests
Of the emperor

The emperor plans to enjoy the world
Without them
The emperor thinks poetry is stupidity
Pencils are gay
God is funny when He recites poetry

The emperor's reality demands that life must not
Go on with poetry
The health of a corrupt government depends on it
There is a speechless hole
In the emperor's heart
The doctors listen
There is no night in the hole
There is no sound in the hole

3.14.97

Byron

I put my hand
Into the dream
That falls upon
The air. It
Touches me a little,
But I don't complain.
I'm almost asleep
When I get there.
Where Byron
Lost the scent of his
Life, over there,
Where the dreams are.
It's always
Hot, like
The eyes of the
Dream. Sometimes
The dream is
On the dunes
Watching the molten
Ocean burn the sun.
The dream scours the
Sand in your fish
Tank for the plastic
Mermaid who is gaining
weight. Nevertheless,
We go to the edge
To watch the dream
And the repetition being
Hurled ashore like
A drop of blue,
You wrote in a poem,
In a language

You alone
Understand
In the dream.

2.26.97

Setting Up a Tombstone

Will you follow my poems into the sea?
This is all I have.
The water in my soul is backing up into
My throat, dragging my heart along with it.

The words arrive with their colorful feathers
Carrying eggs filled with sticky wisdom.
Loaded with seconds and mystery,
Helen steps out of the shower dripping tears:
Her favorite soap.
She doesn't like sun and clouds like I do.
Nevertheless, she's a gardener of green
Rhapsodic money.

Tony Towle is in his "Tomb" shrouded in poetry
Waiting for the phone to ring in a new
Poem from Frank.
Tony will resurrect an inspiration at
Cocktail hour.
Tony's mind is like hot coffee and
Cigarettes in the morning.

"Ten Big Cookies," that's all I need to
Write poetry. David needs ten big chewable
Dictionaries just to get started.
Daniel needs his Mom,
Lindsay, who
Teaches manners to the angels
When they come to Earth.

There is a large farm in my bed.
I raise pencils and paper for *APR*.

I had a cash crop this year
For their American menu:
Lowell on ice. Ginsberg on oxygen.
Kunitz on a bagel. Kumin spread on a thin *mohel*.
Oates sputtering herself with ghee.
Ashbery passing his *Eau de Vie*.

Roberta, my fourth wife is not a dumb blonde.
Nono. She's not.
She keeps my betrayals in an empty room.
She's afraid they'll become likeable
And I'll publish them.
I always knew when she was racing
I could hear the footsteps of my typewriter
Running from the stunning pain.

1.26.97

Waiting For ...

The weather is
peanut blue.
We are swimming
in its cold arms.
The bare branches
are wearing long
winter white
silk opera gloves
that smell like
spring jewelry.
Supernal snow
will turn into
physical rain
the inner life
of flowers that
burn and light
the summer.
Butterflies, the
little books
of dawn, will
reconcile the
June wind as
though we would
live forever,
as we are,
in each other's
eyes.

2.20.97

Frank O'Hara

My heart wears a pair
Of shoes that once belonged
To a young poet.

Whose blood was as fresh
As water.
Whose seatbelt was the hair
Of beautiful women.

Who slept in a thousand dreams
Made of beds.
Who had a friend whose heart
Was a kite tied to a string

Who was eaten by a taxi
Lost on a beach of fire

My dear friend still comes to me
After all these years.
To die once again and to stare
At the holes in my heart.

4.19.98

Heckyll & Jeckyll

Crows see us as another invention.
     Like summer and beauty,
They shimmer at sunrise in their new cars,
     Change their names and color when they see us.
When they fly, they're the bite marks on the sun,
     And nail-scratches of black against the sky.

We matter little to them as we are.
     They prefer hamburger, youth,
Oxygen and mineral water.
     And, of course, we sell our souls to a passing crow,
Because we're shiny things they take to heaven.

Crows are always polite to humans.
     They have lots of money
And live at a party that never ends.
     We're the junk genes they left behind,
That play Aztec football with our heads,
     When we dream and lose.

Crows have relatives everywhere.
     Human warfare moves across the sky
Making more room for them to fly.
     We're just a meal in the next world.
We're the hole in the sky.

Crows are legends and instructors of grace.
     They are the dots in the fog,
And the flight of the uterus.

Crows are the printed warnings
        Of a wasted life.
They will never leave or abandon us.

When we take our last breath,
        Navigating through our mistakes and lies,
The crows will take our last word.

We are the last citizens of a pale race of crows,
        Rearranging the furniture in the mind of God.

Crows turn the planet on its axis when we die,
        And do nothing to the body we'll remember.
Our souls are their meal of the day.

        And the blue marble in its beak,
As it flies away,
        Is the world leaving you.

8.4.99

The Life of Chocolate

To my beloved Helen

We were drowning where the precious fluids were kept, the body and soul
Of gasoline, the Romeo and Juliet of the weather, the lamb curry of our
Dreams, the life of a kiss in the torch of the Statue of Liberty. History and
Biology have crawled away, staring and presuming we will not last as
Long as an American version of eternity. These are the librettos of the

End of time, the manifestos of lean rocks with bony figures that
Encourage time travel when you throw them against the wind, as we
Repeat ourselves like a variety of errors made in the dark, delegating to
The night our personal affidavits, as indentations on the universe. These
Gestures lead to the golden future of time, removing the stars as not to

Obstruct our view. By the end of the future we are covered by a mist,
Signifying the end of a journey once made by children in their
Imagination. This is a pleasant story that has a wonderful ending, but we
Are much too selfish to contemplate the outcome that perhaps may or
May not include us because we have no finishing touches to offer. The

Results are always the same: Save the stock market from the martyrs of
Money. Although the choleric, bearded man with wings will inherit their
Fortune in the end, and eventually squander it on Eastern philosophy and
Artificially colored fast foods. I scratch away at these phenomenal events
Realizing all my life I have been brought to admire the

Accomplishments of a future with you. This remarkable city's economy is
Based on our louche thoughts that continually amaze the imagination of
Chronology. I can see you from my terrace, and many believe you wave
To me when you count champagne bottles, and lovers who pay you with
Oceanic grief. I have always lived and acted with you in mind.

Sometimes I am hungry and think of you eating me for dinner. It takes
Two to do this. As I fly to see you I get too close to the sun to have your
Face scorch my lips before they meet yours. In an hour I will slip into
Another suberic mountainside, hopefully to become your lover once again
For the price of Mexican chocolate. Is it fair to continue flying without

Your lover's letters in hand? My sadness needs them. The ambisinister
Jeweler needs them too. My old ways are changing, like the stories of a
Lake, like the high authority of an arctic night when you are the brightest
Light in the sky. I am stranded without a flat tire to make an excuse to
See this country of broken hearts. Each year, the buried hearts lose

Money on their capital investment, because this diminution is the result of
Sexual desire. This omnipresence tortures the world causing it to explode
From liabilities of remorse. These magic episodes are kept in a vault,
Where I am imprisoned for a crime no one remembers anymore. It is cold
Here and no one comes nor has anyone given me any sustenance since

Nineteen thirty-nine. I am repulsed by the darkness as I am co-owner of
The liveliest days of summer by a pool and it hasn't been the same since
I rehearsed with your scallop shells. They are the bookends of my life,
Shaped like battered oceans where the sea creatures call to each other
By the same name. The other country that is envious of our freedom,

Prosperity, frequent weight gains, and our industrial capacity to mass
Produce soap, has launched nuclear missiles against us. They will be
Greeted like tourists greet the end of the world. Life after death is an
Empty page and it is not fair to turn it more than once. An hour has gone
By and our friend is glowing in the dark somewhere in the Texas desert.

Also, will I be in a state of mind to swallow my end of the bargain, where
The octopus is the greatest criminal who ever lived? Any cartoon will
Verify this propinquity. Look! I'm becoming a cartoon again, with enough
Suckers to hold you forever. The stars still enthrall me because they are

So cold and far away. How can we tell they are as distant as scientists
Claim, if they only appear at night? Nevertheless, what about you

Spending all your time in the depths of the sea playing cards with an 800
Number for fortune telling? Haven't you concluded I cannot move a
Muscle unless you are near me? Do you want me spend the rest of my
Days in the dark? Each time I manage to spy on my dreams you give me
The answer. The only definition I have is on a small private beach

Somewhere holding another ticket to an unbelievable parade of mistakes.
Why were we separated at the heart by those gentle aliens with benign
Grey faces? Didn't you tell them it would be fatal to both of us? They did
Ask you as the overbearing species: Was this a good idea? Who will you
Censure for this tragic medical error for the next millennia? Your hair will
Always sparkle when it snows. I have never known such abundance of

Hair in the dark. A wave of breathlessness consumes the world by
Teenagers dressed like expensive termites. Suddenly the curse is lifted by
A political prisoner who claims he is my half-brother, after I have
Admonished hundreds of them across America and the world. In the end
I scream, admitting I have misused my privacy. My last memory is the

Battle on the last day of the war when I lost the girl of my dreams to a
Hail of bullets meant for me. She loved me until the end, but I could not
Follow her as I was certain I would not be welcomed by her ancestors
Who were the real enemy. She said she would wait for me among the
Foxes. I clung to her last breath as she drove the gas pedal through the

Floor ascending steadily upwards. Before she finally dozed off for the last
Time, she mentioned the beaches she would miss. She said to me she
Would not need ice for her daily glass of white wine and was going to
Celebrate splitting with my lock-step emotions. She said she was dying
For love, not for me. I continued to act as if I were deeply hurt.

This performance became a way of life for me. I stopped drinking,
Smoking and reaming of migraine headaches, even lost some weight
Becoming a graphic caricature to impress other women. But now I am
Seeking religious closure to my lustful pursuits, not repentance. I often
Wonder why my life has been this way. It would have been much

Different if I were born without a body, only a burlap bag filled with
Autumn leaves, with a very small head on top. None of this would have
Happened, just difficulty breathing resulting from chronic hay fever.
NASA would have collected prayers from schoolchildren all over America

And astronauts would have taken
Me up into outer space,
So the angels could hear me better.

7.17.01

The Unbearable Truth

We watch each other like a bad cough,
      And smile like firemen being photographed
For doing something vague and good. Our hands fidget
      In our pockets with something secret and tragic.
We're going to penetrate the truth with deadly accuracy.
      The result will be the grandest defection:
The eternal cauterization of the truth!
      Truth is a ghost with eyes as wide as ships.
There is no limit to the lies an old truth can tell.
      Everything it wears is minus the details of both
Good and bad. The travails of truth travel
      Faster than nostalgia, the stars and the pain of a broken heart.
Truth is an old tree that looks like God,
      With a pair of bells as cold as a museum.
Truth is at the bottom of the sea,
      Has one tooth and can't read and aspires to be a tongue.
Truth is the scariest door in a Hollywood movie.
      Truth is a mummy cursing at a dial tone.
So long as you live, lies will serve you,
      And crumble into dust when you tell the truth.

8.5.99

Afterlife

There are never enough beds
To go around the stars.
I keep these things to myself,
As the moon keeps
A vast collection of shoes.

There is a time clock inside of me
You keep punching out,
To stop me from dreaming.
These travels have no future.
Like the establishment,

I was once aftershave and anticipation.
Everything began there,
With its artifacts and oblivion.
But I still prefer the daydream with its agenda,
And the afterlife of fingers,

Taking my measurements.
Alas, I am done for the day and have a few requests:
Perhaps some fried squid to unclutter the mind where all roads end.
Or some aromatic sleep with its beautiful crescent pillows.
And a book with long legs that tells where to begin.

7.6.99

After the Greek Restaurant

Dreams never heal themselves, they were not told it was not cheap.
That they themselves were the lesions of pleasure and pain,
That they could not heal their own cloudy skin. Their divine mission is the
Sleeping memory, the one without the sermon of the torso by our side.

Still, you have left the eye of beauty behind to check my days and
Moments, never to mistake a beginning from an ending again,
From false marching bands playing promises to the wind,
Arias without lipstick, beach houses with no depths or sustenance from

The sun. What about my romantic snoring in your ear after the Greek
Restaurant? What if I met you in my new slippers made from your own
Hair that I collected with the sweat from my lips during a moment of
Romantic aestival. Will the stars let us sleep again on the mantle

That some arthritic called a bed? According to what history has to tell,
There are no goodbyes or people at the bottom of the ocean waiting to be
Rescued. It is abandonment that will read to us when we dream.
Do not let me hang around because we are not there to greet it

With our differences. Look at the past as it destroys itself on our customs
That reverse the stories of mothers and fathers.
Since no love is complete without a chill,
The less noise we make, the better.

7.28.02

A Comfort Station

It all comes down to the color of your shoelaces and how you vibrate
When you tie them in the afternoon.
Strange, how so many things are remembered in one day,
How many lifetimes will ride the subway with you in mind?
I have thought of you as an enchanted cave where spells came to meet,

To practice their Latin while doing their make-up in a magic mirror
Specializing in the profound reflections of love.
I have strawberries and a piña colada for you when you disrobe your
Consciousness to seduce the facts of the tarot cards.

They are not eager to look back,
They are only interested in the objects of a pleasing future to be delivered
Like an orgasm in a teenage barn where secrecy sparkled,
Where on a windless day the hay was still and at peace before our arrival.
The mice and the owls among the eves would agree we were a

Cacophonous race of lovers who were capable of intelligent speech,
Like wolves lamenting the moon.
Something has to happen to our arms who miss us,
Something simple like forgiveness, something as clear as a kiss before you
Go from here to there in your travels to inspect the troops in the fields

Of loved ones. If not, something will come into being to remember us.
O, don't you see how experimental an empirical life is when you are not
Around to inspect the bathrooms I have just sanitized in your honor?
Look at the shining face of the kitchen floor as it squints up at your silent
Underpinnings of infinite, sizzling mystery, to name a few.

All I can do is think of evolution and the sky around you.
What happens is you get the offshore breeze of the universe as I become

An overused star in a castle infested with vices from the past.
Morality is jettisoned into an uncertain future where the last word is silent
And never heard when we sleep.

7.31.02

Alligator of Happiness

I ride the subway with all these bare-breasted faces.
To my eternal discredit,
They remind me of my five-minute life,
Pounding against my heart.

My fantasy is I am a loitering hunter
Of nudes who ride the subways,
With eyes that crack the light of men who stare.
The nudes are beautiful white ants in the darkness,
Blowing coins and leaves at me.

My technique is familiar and simple conversation,
Rhyming bad words that have little meaning.
They accumulate like cities in Iceland.
The words are flames and I am their lycanthropy.
The riders pretend I do not exist.

But I eventuate like the law of someone's
Humanity I will never cheat.
These are hungry old habits,
The voyeurs of childhood,
We allow to run our lives as adults.

Still, I wait for them,
Like the alligator of happiness,
With a bouquet of senile flowers.
They finally appear like birds from the Nile.
I have kept this appointment all my life.

4.15.99

Juarez

These empty words are so remote. They are stories someone wants
To believe at the end of the century. Everyone gathers their sea of telluric
Pain to greet the beginning of the new world.

Cars stop and watch the deck chairs limp across the street to await
The coming of the new year. It is the end of summer and autumn and
Winters and springs, and panzer infatuation.

After four hundred eighty-one years, I cannot pull out the Spanish arrow
In my eye. Suddenly everything I knew was inhuman:
The oceans, the tadpoles in their new cars. The clams became
Cheerleaders. The palm trees, strippers, and everyone forgot
Deer are the shapes of God.

His official language became Latin, when he ceased to be a Jew,
Biting his nails and collecting cans like a cheap minister with sunny gold teeth.
The tender years that once wore oysters would never speak to Him again.

The female spider became a lesbian, devouring our new long legs,
That would never again climb the toy steps our fathers left us. Although
Our legs are hairy and the lilies of a theater, the gentle lips of
Our pyramids rest on our souls like a lover's fingers.

How many aspirins will we take to reach the surface of truth?
My existence is for sale. The dawn is learning English.
The waves of the sea are unionizing.

The stones that were once our troubled hearts are eating chocolate.
I come to sell you fish, the bread in my blood and my existence.

10.17.99

Ode to Things About Destiny

(In pursuit of Kenneth's Destiny)

Why should I keep you up all night babbling about destiny?
Elephants know it is an old idea,
Terrified of small things like being alive.
Will destiny send my computer flowers when it dies?
Will destiny notice I'm wearing new underwear?
Does destiny get angry when women undress,
Exposing their wings?
Destiny can be as cold as an abandoned car,
Or as rewarding as sleeping late.
Sometimes destiny is a clock in a tropical hotel where it's never late.
We make plans and destiny laughs
Like Dracula sucking the minutes out of tomorrow.
The mission of destiny is not to get dirty when you make a wish,
Because it's having breakfast with tomorrow,
And sticking a fork in your wishes.
O dearest humanity,
It will never give you a gold star for good behavior.
Destiny can hear the bees laughing.
Destiny is traditional: It does not think of you,
But you constantly think of it.
It knows you as well as your tongue knows the inside of your mouth
When in love with long sentences.
That's when destiny's doors open like the womb
Welcoming you with flames and seeds.
Destiny will come ashore with warrants and lovers,
Take your hand and sell you in the dark,
The reporters will be waiting at the funeral:
Who is destiny? Is it male or female?
What is destiny's favorite position? Does it have big breasts?
In the end, destiny will take you out with a bazooka, anyway.

It has something for everybody,
And you won't come back.
Destiny will deliver your Buddhist regrets,
To the mystified Old Man who has never heard of a holiday. Finito!

12.5.99

The Daily Nose

There are many kinds of lovers in the world, I assume I am one of them.
However, once I started looking between your legs for the last rung to
Success on the ladder to the future, I became an unemployed gnome as I
Stared into the household darkness looking for divinities and the powers
Of heaven. Instead I was hooked and afraid of becoming lonely, hungry

And tired as they say in those smoky rooms of recovery where everyone
Smokes on a respirator listening to organ music.
Bystanders are not allowed to speak unless they have lost a fortune to the
Addictions of life. Being alone is a groundbreaking characteristic of
Enlightenment and obscurity, because no one knows you are around.

Nevertheless, you did in your quest for a Homeric scenario of oregano and
Spinach. As couples, we were the tableaux of the week when we took
Italian dance lessons of pasta. The dance teacher accused me of
Fathering her slow-witted son as his hair was as black as mine:
Her husband looked on in befuddlement taking his temperature to make

Sure his hearing was not impaired by her statement.
Speaking of the past, it's time that the fates reward me with a pleasant
Day in bed and a harmonious love life and an empathic female therapist in
A short skirt that barely escapes my vision of recuperation.
I often wonder, was this incident a premonition of her because you

Seemed so happy when I looked up your skirt wearing my parachute?
No doubt I will go on dreaming privately to myself of your bad judgment
And misdirected inspirations, but in the end my fate will be worse than
Death itself, that bleached backdrop to sleep,
Here my snoring interposes, hopefully in your ear,

For I will be a long-retired lover who can preview the relentless facts of
The past that will not be about your state of being,

But soon will. I have enjoyed your health care prognostications of daily
Reality we occupied with its impressive denouncements of hope.
You do not know how well off you are the center of this immense

Conspiracy of the human epic as a highly mechanized baby machine.
I'm just Cortez calling from the Sperm Bank of Spain asking you for a
Warm renewal and deposit slip to a good detective story.
The plot and especially the ending were always yours to decide,
Just pull the lever and wait for the rush of air to go by.

1.22.02

Blue Postcard from the Fjords

And death put down his fork to admire the fixtures of earth,
The tyrannies of sleeping, and the ten reasons we are unkind to each
Another. These story book illustrations are plain enough to the onlookers
Who have never had a life-threatening experience or genuine affection
Toward some desirable stillness of thought,

When unaware of the imagined proliferation of past mistakes.
I frequently come to this stop, to take a pause from my daily migrations
To stay ahead of fatigue and the resulting heady conclusions that defeat
My anticipated freedoms that wash away all the evening stops and fading
Triumphs that occur just before one falls asleep.

People historically wave to us as we leave the station.
I presume they are well-meaning gestures that remind one of all those
Plaster acrobats hanging from the walls of Catholic churches.
I force on you a blue postcard of an aging couple standing nude in a
Partially frozen fjord that reminds me of the future and how things should

Be at that stage in one's life.
I mean, how they are holding hands and facing each other for the last
Time, not caring that Dante is becoming impatient trying to keep the cold
Drafts out and the conversation as simple as possible,
Weather permitting on the surface of the world where the inhabitants are

Oblivious of their pending circumstances.
It has to be this way for the waters to hold hands coming to the surface
Like the bubbles of the heart when you call about dinner and the trivia
Of people's movements when thinking of the intimate details in the
Changing rooms of gossip. "My, look at that," and all the smoke of doubt

Blows away in another day of imagined, romantic calisthenics that will
Melt away any thoughts of being stranded with the wrong person whose

Soul is a human fish you never intended to bend to your will.
Tragic and foolish choices aside, there are not enough pillows or
The moon to begin our lesson.

9.14.02

My Blue Agave

With your kind thoughts I am excused from my life, which is the grand
Dwarf whom poetry serves only when it pleases to do so.
I will make magic into perfect justice for you, the stranger among many.
The power to enchant comes from a brief moment at a party of friends
And late lovers. Your calm eyes are lucid—proof of a secret disorder that

Worships despondency with the lone master who drinks at the other end
Of the bar with the malingerers and past historical deeds that made goodness
An offense and a bore to the deceased. The reliable newsprint from hell
Says that vertigo and fig leaves are eaten with compulsive laughter.
So be frank about your health and how often you change the sheets.

I will always need your delicate freedom and your imagined four-letter
Words that I chose to be like the casualties of old men chasing young
Ankle bracelets. You are not malicious by nature as I am,
Perhaps I am the result of good will gone astray in youth,
When my thoughts were the walls of my life,

Keeping me here to stay. Finally when you appeared like sunlight on a
Quiet windowsill where nothing would grow such as youth, love,
Not even the past with its infestations of dying young and famous.
Nevertheless, I am here and I really exist decades away from being
Famous and I have actually grown an inch skyward away from the sacred

Blood they talked about in the Spanish movies.
What is dreadful is I will never see them again in paradise or the tropics.
When I dream again, I will be resting in a chair shaped like you,
And a shadow of what I was. You will be the wind in my eyes,
Which will not tear any more in the quiet garden where suffering becomes

The sun, with or without a day upon which to shine.
I never suspected truth could be so simple,

Although you spoke of it this way, often, during our daily hiatuses from
Romantic civility in order for the moment to lose consciousness.
Yet I was too busy with my nobility,

Nonsense and what the heavens would think of as sunshine
And moonlight, fidgeting with the middle of the afternoon.
Here come the firefighters and the Spartans with their solemn faces of
Ossified honor. They are coming for us, for we are their frigid
Acquisitions and cannot sleep.

King Lear

To my son

I'll carry you home in my death to protect the days I spent with you.
When you were born, I became the tsar of fathers.
I built battleships and gunboats to protect your cribs from the dark ikon
Of birth and sour cherries. I was the huge fish who kept you in its mouth
Away from the sharks; the friendly fisherman who hid behind your
Grandmother's piano. I gave you the secrets of the sea believing they were
Words of wisdom. Now I am an upturned boat in your heart, pelted by
Every word you speak. However, the old fishermen sent a word to shout to
Me that children fade when they themselves have children, who say to their
Parents "We're men and we are back." "We will grow as tall as a piano."
"What will I do with you as tall as a piano?" "Be sensible, we're going to be
the emperor of pianos, and you'll be a monk in a childhood tale, again."

Before the World Ends

Sometimes a spider's thread will appear like some magical human organ,
The young woman of your dreams, or your favorite shirt.
Nevertheless, it is time for a Sunday morning instead of the secret room
We share with the end of sorrow: The bleeding label on the heart is
Already tomorrow to the evening stars that appear tame as they watch

Our unadulterated atrocities and benign cruelties inside the name of a
Marble wedding cake with the tower of Babel on the top.
This audacious confection was made with a million nails that represent
The strawberry-colored past of someone's life you envied.
That is how this world began, like a funny little bright spot in the sky.

Someone was crazy enough to make a calendar to follow it around the
Impetuous forms of poetry to map our lives when there was nothing else
To do with our time alone, when the pages of our thoughts are turned by
A golden dust that can only be found on the horizon of sleepy thoughts as
They leave the unmade bed of the mind. In this flood the meaning of life

To you is clear but goes away too soon with your common existence in
Hand. We live in this contrived ruin with plastic statues of ourselves in
Painful distress because the stars have lost their patience with us.
Time is running out, and we are no longer their destiny,
Their travel guide to the heavens,

Pages too heavy with life for the wind to fly onto another world.
This poem is the wallpaper of a colorless small history,
Too dense and off-color to hang anywhere to be seen.
It is always about you and my period of adjustment,
I start every day early before I leave the house to insure I get a seat on

The subway so that I may clear my head of my nightly distractions that
Conspire against me on closer examination.
Doing anything during the argument between night and day is difficult for
Me as to who should come first to channel our history into the uniform I
Can wear for you to promptly inspect before the world ends.

3.17.01

After You There Is Poetry

In this irreversible state there are no covenants so let me die singing to
The obscure notes of somewhere else archaic
And beautiful where there is no unpleasant respiration only the darkness

Between infinity and a word that is a dream that celebrates God's
Birthday. It said, "Let there be you, made of me and old poets that will
Die like violins with broken hearts."

I was dipped in chocolate for you,
Don't floss me and let me be true pleasure.
Autumn is the flag that defeated the summer of fertility and memorized

The color of our severed kisses inch by inch.
I am yours like a bird's warm memory of spring. My father gave me a
Vision so I could swim inside you.

11.19.01

The Body of Prayer

After David Shapiro

In another life the popular fish dream of water and sacred bread as they
Emerge from a synagogue like familiar cantors that were forbidden to
Touch the hand of God, who is not in attendance while they sing.

To speak a prayer seems insolent to the women shaped like the aisles in
Heaven. The angels are not permitted to sing, as they are not returning
To earth with the entomology of music that the rabbi dispenses

Like sacred bread. This bread is not serious nostalgia like the taxonomy
The Talmud prescribes. The great cantor wonders why are we dead
And still suffering. Will we that serve the dead in their quest return to

Sing again for their sins? The common self-lacerations of Kierkegaard will
Come to us like those pauperized in the desert.
The rabbi is the bee of the synagogue and the boss of bosses of the song
Of forgiveness. He emits a little candlelight for the dead to see their way.

10.20.01

Each Morning Takes Longer to Get Here

Is it true we are what we lose in the darkness of being,
In the wonder of the supernatural moment when touched by the loving
Ordinary touch? Teach me how the years will end,
And how seriously the fray will rule the miracle of timid faith.
You always knew I would return like the moment of the first love with its

Ageless pyramids of romantic slaves.
I am waiting for the answer with its web of circumvented increments and
Its fragmentary truths that are withheld out of embarrassment because
You are from heaven. The connective tissue that once held the wind in
My heart is beyond recognition as it twists and turns in its sleep.

It is only you that matters to the warm soup of the universe with its bread
And hungry stars. It needs another chapter in our lives complete its
Inactivity, otherwise we will be a pause in its path and conversations with
The tree of life. When the beloved leaves eternity,
Civilization returns the bounty of affection and replenishes the rivers

And oceans with the hands of gods. These historical machines are as
Wide as the blue breast of the birds of truths and the universe.
We will rest here, no one will mind our stopping for a rest to eat our
Pungent delinquencies that satisfy the hunger of the adolescent
Imagination. Finally, here at Versailles, among the eloquent debacle and

The buffet of colorful aviarists, I no longer know who I am or what I look
Like since I left with the poster of the lingering paradigm that the dog
Steals from me as I sleep in the hut by the edge of the great city of
Answers. I listen for you to come for me,
But it seems each morning takes longer to get here.

2.11.02

The Public Health of the Heart

At the end of each praetorial epoch the bounty of consciousness changes
Hands with the previous half of my stay here with you, unlocking the
Mysteries of expectancy in my world. How I envy the infected glories of
Your childhood and the triumphant father fighting the gods with your
Youth in hand and the shield of the future in the other that would heal all

Your days to come. And just as twilight was upon us re-evaluating our
Fortunes I became ill with not knowing who I was despite your selfless
Transfusion of maturity that I found difficult to conjugate,
Descanting its lustrous tale of happiness. No power on earth can deny my
Ritual mistakes of imperious desire and statistical delays of confessional

Happiness that is as simple as salt on the table of joy, despite its danger
Of boredom and the unromantic chores of living for endless moments of
Incoming disappointments I imagined would destabilize the power of
Our unmitigated understanding of longing for a fantastic tale as sad
As childhood decay. I have come full circle like a predictable supernatural

Boomerang being thrown at a mosquito with a lion's head. But now our
Extinction is eminent in the scheme of pleasant memories and we will no
Longer think like a single organism that delighted the gods with our
Impromptu foolishness and lavish perpetual doting on an
Endangered species of stars that turn the pages of the universe.

2.13.02

Wreckage du Jour

Wreckage has a way of perpetuating itself like distance and fear do when
You are lost, or cannot sleep. That is when candles talk like dragons in
The dark in the throat of the wreckage we have left behind for someone
Else to torment with other memories. I do everything with them in hand,
Including making love to my seductive cello and talking to your fish.

The most pleasurable things always happen in the dark by the sound of
The trains leaving to explore the horizons in my head where I am a
Toothache in the living space of my actions. There, the life forms we
Once loved wait for our return to bloom, adding moisture to our tired
Organs, once the flames of our delicate existence that we took for granted

With auspiciousness of youth. Is it the same on other worlds?
According to those calamitous myths of creation, it must be so, as an entity
In its own right, the moon is a ball of wreckage meant for lovers to
Stare at during its fullness on hot summer nights. This is called
The human condition that lays dormant until puberty, and spring

Intercedes with sparkling irrationality. These tiny creatures of desire
Wreck havoc on our nervous systems as ants do to human vegetation,
With small bites to the heart that become lacerations of endearment
Lasting a lifetime if the subject is willing to endure and live out this rock
Opera called "The Grand Vagina," sharing the seasons and its rivers,

Submitting to its edible seeds to become lumbering lovers who will claim
To see beyond Mars, to the wondering asteroids, where affections are
Undisturbed. These emotions are uncontaminated by our arrogant
Locomotion. As usual, the onlookers form a circle of admiration as we
Exaggerate our basic lives, pounding it into the future of wreckage.

10.7.01

Autobiography

The wine was poured out of a flower that wore gloves,
Reminiscent of the surgical gloves worn by the army bombing
Disreputable foreigners. It will be an important apostasy in the burial
Chambers below the grand achievements.
My dreams spend their off-hours at a singular factory that

Manufactures windows of women always undressing in the dark.
This is the wonderment of national daydreaming without
The possibility of being interrupted by the imminent exclamations
From a previous life. These are the signs of an ancient French sexuality
i.e. Every female citizen will be in chains for fifteen minutes on a chosen

Holiday, called lament. Classic beauties for those pagan memories that
Pursue us in the twilight of the subway when you are being squeezed into
A ball by Cronos himself whose internal organs are made of gold
And comets. I usually fall asleep wishing for the good old days before
Shaving cream in a can and propellants were invented for the weariness

Of the new world in a state of unendurable passion,
Faking the most natural elements of the human condition.
I am confined to the inferior organs of a marble statue while
Justice and honor are in a coma of issues and regression.
I have endured the oppressive policy of angels and their portents of my

End. Will the seraphs with dates in their hair grant my last wish before
Oblivion? In the end, we will fall from a high place, resembling aluminum
Foil Christmas tears glittering in the sun, you will find me in the throes of
My last vision of romantic daydreaming and assimilate the prologue of my
Autobiography with these omnivorous culinary scribbles.

10.10.01

The World as Red as Wine

Nevertheless, this hiatus is for you, with its graceful maps
And romantic equilibriums. How much is there to waiting?
There is not enough for two:
A one-way destination of colorless illusions on the baggage cart.

I will be civil to your Chinese fighting fish and I will not overcook the
Broccoli rabe. Have we forgotten our daily walks today?
No, it has forgotten us on its way to the stars with our marzipan
Memories covered with disquieting Turkish fig leaves.

I keep the stairs to heaven in my wallet with my son's photograph,
You can join us whenever you wish or find the time between migraines
And pagan accountings. The sciatica is no longer in my imagination,
It has moved out and up to the center of my chest claiming it is the heart

I wished for after the car accident. Let me memorialize my
Thoughts of you for another time of bucolic accessibility.
Your thoughts have so much to say to me but wander away into the fog
That keeps the monkeys silenced during their arboreal rituals of feasting

Their eyes on the onlookers who are as strange as the trees in heaven.
Perhaps life will be better with you in bed where zippers are antediluvian,
As hysterical inventions and we are the outdoors of each other's skin.
My night poems will drone on for centuries without respite

Or moisture to survive the milky pounding of solitude.
I continue to recede like the inventor of the pencil.
What keeps me going is the fear of bliss,
Your last word in my ear.

10.20.02

After Reading the Cards

Poetry is the eye of the earth, all the rest is imaginary
And wishful thinking for a better place where the thing you love is not an
Illusion or a gift that was lost with the Titanic,
Where the silence and clowns laugh behind our backs at day's

End when we count how many subway tokens tomorrow will require,
How many false smiles will be dispatched by the flesh of the Devil.
Stay with me, dear one, while I pack my words for the next world
Where they originally came from, where I found you among the olive

Trees and sour cream. I started with little deserving little when I was
Dropped here. I was on my way to somewhere else when my flight was
Interrupted by terrorists brandishing my reveling wishes.
I am glad the other character with the capital letter at the beginning does

Not pay attention to me anymore or to my romantic dreaming;
Look where it has gotten the world.
I am glad I did not recover my kingdom,
I am glad to have time to write to you so that,

Alas, I can believe I have lived, and will not die suspended between
Dreams and wishes like the others who live on the other side of the wall.
Deeply, I've been blessed, I have not lost my quest for another day with
You, nor have my hands let go the wheel your father clings to.

For under your spell I am the retina of heaven and the thoughts of flying
Autumn leaves in pursuit of the lonely and unhappy books that never get
Read because their counsel was not available for breathing,
Only to those that see into the future.

9.30.02

To Live by Night with You

I have kept the old thoughts to live by, and to learn things from them,
Every day. The cardinal city has not changed, the cheeses no longer ripen
There like they used to,
Watermelons and honey have lost their color for life in the sun.
Feta refuses to come to the dinner table with our favorite myths.

Racks of lamb and slices of lemon do their loving in the lair of gossip
Without us to dine with.
In this old city the moon will set without us in hand,
It has no other place to go. Will I be elected again to comfort the old ways
Of nature when we sleep with the strange news of hope?

I like what you have left me with, the black tentacles of innocence with
Their vivid cruelty that we defend strapped to indecision.
There is still enough for two to live on:
What dreaming calls imagination, the hors d'oeuvres of the soul,
That tend to our sleepless nights.

Do you have enough for two?
I will leave in the morning on the tintinnabulations of the horizon, just as
You predicted. But I preferred to be a bat enmeshed in the black
Macaroons in your hair to keep the light from disfiguring the codicils
And addendums of imagination. Why complain about the way kisses are

Organized in the streets? This is a small town for siestas to be free
And at peace with their inquiring hands. Nothing is more resilient than
The afternoon sun on the bedroom window to oversee our breathing to
Each other as the bed follows our steps to heaven that comes to us from
All directions. On the way, life manages to dispel all its fears of hidden

Pleasures. This is life moving over the skin of the earth,
Imagining we are a wonderful book for lovers,

A manual of constant events in the chemistry of things to come
For holidays keep track of their own events to remind us
There is a night and day to live by.

7.14.02

Catching My Breath

Dear, will I ever breathe again? It is obscene to forgive a machine in the
Clouds that stops when it is denied gold and red wine, and we accept the
Graces of sponges soaked in vinegar. Faith is put to the question as if
Treason grew on shameless trees which are far too damaged to repair.

With some humor and humility the railroad will end here where the
Station was once erased with the shards of blue hope that were a bed
Where our imagining slept with the same dream that has not aged with
Memory. But it grieves without our presence for it is cold in the ruins

Where the rain has no place to collect desires. My flesh is Adam waiting
For his glory, or a weakness dying of pity and lack of wrath. I heard
Orpheus sing to us over his favorite lunch of rice and squash. He does
Not eat meat when he is in love, catching his breath that accompanies

You irrevocably because Lucifer is envious and wants to change his life to
Match yours. I was at his extravagant trail on the fifth world of sinners
Where inspiration spoke of birth and love and condemned time when my
Brain becomes vacant and sorrow is unshaven. We will not pay and still

Attend the epoch when the night comes harboring promises on another
Universe where the three wise dolphins spent their summers with the
Philistines in the quiet darkness of myths. How will you look at me at the
End of the jackpot when everything of major importance is reduced to a

Confronting last glance? Will I shatter like a pyramid in your ageless eyes?
Will I refuse my chance when the pentacratic riddle shrieks in the havens
To join the operatic offenses in someone else's notion of farewell duet?
Will you sing to me on your swing of white wine, inebriating the birds on

Their flight to spring? My love, I say, this is the way it will always be as I
Grow a kiss in my hand for us to take on vacation for I will lose my way
When I look at you across our table. Yes, the one with the sails in the
Gene pool of the Northern Lights.

10.31.02

Felonies and Arias of the Heart

I need more time, a simple day in Paris hotels and window shopping.
The croissants will not bake themselves and the Tower of London would
Like to spend a night in the tropics with grey sassy paint. It has many
Wounds and historic serial dreams under contract to Hollywood.
Who will play the head of Mary, Queen of Scots, and who will braid her

Hair? Was it she who left her lips on the block for the executioner,
Whose hands would never find ablution, who would never touch a woman
Again or eat the flesh of a red animal. Blood pudding would repulse him
Until joining Anne. That is the way of history written for Marlow and
Shakespear. They are with us now that we are sober and wiser,

Not taking the horrors of poetry too seriously. Why am I telling you this
Nonsense, when I have never seen you sip your coffee or tea,
In the morning? Not to mention,
Never heard you sing, although some claim it is quite grand.
Will you teach me to sing like Chaliapin? Will I impress you with my

Cartoon Russian accent? I like sour cream and borscht;
We went to school together. My minor was caviar and blinis.
This is what it means to listen to Boris Godunov late at night.
Cool mornings are for Lakmé and songs of flowers for misplaced lovers.
But why should we speak in a foreign language to each other,

We are not birds. I have other stories too strange and beautiful to be
Told. They have no sound or memory. They will rest on your lips when
You bring your hands to your mouth to stop their gush of air against your
Face. We should go back and meet again at the street fair of cufflinks.
Our hearts teach us how to fly with wings of pain.

That is the price of the disarticulated lessons we should not abstain from
Playing. The accumulated misdemeanors add up to the most egregious
Felony: Ignoring the demands of the heart. We remain in abeyance to
The muses who are only interested in their outcomes,
We are just the worms on their hooks of selfishness.

What do they care, we are not Greek. We are just a dream of pleasant
Comic arias that suffice as whims in the morning.
We are small enemies to them with strange large hearts that control the
Weather in the heavens. They cannot change or unteach us not to
Trespass their quarters of endowment. Perhaps, after all, you are an

Affable spirit bubbling over with your own deductions to minimize the
Pointed dots in your beautiful endeavors.
Although I feel like a bird with a broken wing,
Each day I think of you I fumble an attempt to fly to impress you with
The color of my paper wings.

9.23.02

Appetizer

I hope we don't remain this far from the sea, the consommé of wishes
that we cautiously wade into when it is crystal clear and the impurities
and their consequences become the austerity in our floating lives in the
aquarium of aqueous truth. Salvation never feels a need to absolve itself.
It's always too involved watching our most enjoyable retreats where the
ancient courtesy began to exploit our imprinted indolence that mistakenly
was interpreted as the steam of innocence distinguishing the truth from
out and out charismatic revenge. So we only have seconds to be buried,
before the great fan swats us away to what some say is a better place to
chew the cuds of our grandest imperious ruminations. Although no one
has ever made contact to us from there, rumors persist that it is over
rated, to say the least, it is the preferred place to dream and analyze
previous shortcomings and pleasurable dysfunctions that were never
intended to injure anyone but a childhood lover, who is now the president
of an oil rich country in a deserts of camels and flies. Why would you
want to go there, anyway? You can drink and smoke all you want,
never get drunk, never cough in the mornings and no bad breath either.
Just dreary, repetitious days with no painful accents to keep you going in
the heavenly gutters of dull peace. These are the offensive omens of a
normal life, *sans sal*, and suddenly you will find yourself running into a wall
with a lance firmly imbedded with your name on its shaft. Stay with me
and share the yams, the vitamin pills, the seltzer water and the double
lamb chops. We will embezzle the sun and go anywhere we please with
the guarantee of good weather. You've got to decide on what finger
you'll wear the decoding ring. Well, dear lady, I have lowered the
drawbridge for you and your silk solitude that does not appear to suffer
any wear and tear. I enjoy your buzzing in my head and your polite
catcalls and the attendant humor that I suspect amuses you about 1 AM
in the morning after steeping tea with your crowded brain as company in
the dark. I don't remember when I wrote this.

The Blessed

For David Shapiro, my very best friend

Why am I worthy of this mystery, I am not a prodigious sinner,
I don't have the time anymore: There are commemorations and odes
That have committed nameless enormities while forgetting their dinner of
Consonants and overcooked pronouns. You have only to watch the

Mouths of the agents to realize how squalid and untidy creation is with all
Its words that amount to three hundred species of snake, one dynasty of
Commas and one declarative seraph without speech. What is really at the
Bottom of the ocean is an epiphany of beliefs we will never recite or swim

With on the surface. At the bottom, no one gets turned away,
No one because here this is equal to the abnegation of living.
The day is too long for short trances and telling the future what to do
About the past. The public has been wrecked with faceless words.

The hands are out nightclubbing
And the angels are finally watching the stars in the shower,
The dead poets are sleeping calmly and will no longer harm the language.
The Madonna with the heavy Israeli accent is wearing a torn glove

Holding asparagus, so we can keep our crucial updates of the Crusades to
Buy bigger cars. Poetry is twisted from our skin and dedicated to an
Aging memory because the countdown is not very far away anymore,
And the seconds are priceless and enjoying the view

And the diamonds we caught up in the bed of the world, when it was
Correct to sleep with someone's long hair to become a member of love,
A member of Jerusalem, a light with a heart that no one could break with
A kiss but with the mathematics of poetry.

Blessed is the green and red light that invented us,
More so, blessed is the highway that lets us write,
And blessed are the poets who invented us as poets.

11.13.02

Dolphins in the Dark

You are the fifth and final act in my life, perhaps the grandest of my
Indiopathic choices: Nirvana and melodies under an angle's wing.
The demons told you, he's a bad copy of what you want and deserve in
Paradise. Take him out of the machine or it will never copy again!
So it goes with religion, empathic events, and fortune-telling cards
And old razor blades. The weak spirited are cambium to disappointments
And his word is like any other word in a newspaper of underground
Seductions. This is an illness of low voices and grasshopper hearts that
Come and go with the diseases of spring.
All a snake can do is listen to a tender breast,
As the legend of Cleopatra is a vivid recurring dream in the sand beds of
The sun. Will my ten-foot doodles in the dark talk to you in the dark?
The echogram in your womb is not me but my poem in the dark.

11.13.02

Someone Else's Memory

For this and all the land masses more private than a dream, even more
Secretive than want, it is evident all is subordinate to this elegant
Function with its reams of typing paper and bullheaded dictionaries.
Here my watch turns silence into light and to vast pools of poetry.

I wish my public face could join yours since fate has made each of us our
Prehistory where our bones will be kept as periapts and talismans of good
Fortune to lovers passing by, holding hands, in doubt of their mongrel
Instincts and voices from the hired symphony that plays weird ubiquity

Affection. Forgetting that this would be heartless
Underdeveloped craft turned into an all-expense played trip to
Nowhere or into an apartment with narrow rooms of mornings that
Mingle with our habits of waking with a handful of Hindu pleasures.

I should like to become your day to day proclamations, to hear
Your speech, envy your shadow when the lights are on and thrill to
Finding you in the dark. You get my drift of things to do after the mission
Comes for us like a cloud with dragons' teeth.

When the fumes are discharged we will belong to the tender
Terms of perfection that will turn us inside out as if we were the climaxes
Of introspection and emotions. Only then will our description make
Sense to the viewers with the marked fingers who can feel the

Phenomenal density of the future, because we will be there to greet
Them on their quest to fill the bags of loneliness.
Although I am an intruder, I mean your kind no harm.
My barefooted diaspora is annoying and my ad hoc interpretations of

Areas are limited but immediate, if we discuss who belongs to
Who in these infinite serials on the black and white screen, where we
Officially belong, where we left our baggage to be radiated for feelings by
The naïve inventor of our contact lenses. You should not be aghast at my

Waggling tail, I only use it for dusting and scarring my students when
They don't pay their dues to me. The theme begins to bleed, it cannot
Attach itself to anything because it does not know how all this began on
The magic staircase of first meetings and glances. All the little monsters

Were on TV watching us through the introductions. Was it your hungry
Leopard dress or your dark owl earrings that would end my distractions?
Or your lack of interest in my hospice with its tales of sunshine that drove
Me to this incantation. Surely it was you behind the curtains

With my life on your hips when it all began to fall apart as I watched
Things in your eyes fleet back and forth like an unpaid journey.
So I am lost without an eye in someone's memory who does not
Remember what I look like.

11.26.02

Archives du Jour

This is the end of the classical consommé of vices, nonetheless,
The census will not change the things I have to say to you.
Think of these lines to you as birds returning to their place of origin.

But at certain times in the history of events in the universe,
The rotation of the earth betrays the weather and the phone rings
And I realize I am lost with no destination of my own to return to on any

Given sunny day. And I am lost in the luxurious curly hair of night,
Pulsing like the light of the stars. There are no beaches here, only sandy
Skin burning without the orchestra of the sun shedding its romances.

You look so different tonight on this planet where everyone wears
Telegrams to bed in order to alleviate their sexual inhibitions, the ones
That are always on sale, because night's approaching footfalls

Refuse to leave the sandbox that we maintain as a wedding bed.
Have you noticed every time I start nibbling on something, thinking it is
You, my shoes turn into gold wings and I streak across the sky like

Apollo did when he saw you bathing in milk.
This vision cuts me in two while the furniture is arranged
By gods who canceled our leases to the future.

12.28.01

"This is a Wonderful Ballad"

You alone are here moving time out of the way when it burst into tears.
Peach blossoms fall to the earth becoming meaningful moments of
Cocainized eternity. The crime of living is Virgilian melancholy where our
Past is a barbed-wire fence guarding a road that stretches far into the
Distance where happiness is not a threat to children but a repository for
Sad adults. Our despair is a classical Greek event when we finally bury
The loudspeakers without knowing we are the opening seasons of its pity,
That ours is not pain abnegation, that the wounds will not miss our
Indulgent attentions, especially in the city that survives in the dark.
Even at this carbon that is your future hand in mine as we bury our
Careworn dead, who need as much rest as we do for what we are,
Have become, will become holding the appendages of reason that are
Rooted in the heart just beneath the searchlights that we ourselves keep
Alight for summative, artificial introspection to name the emperors of
Meaning, who are the days of the month in that country, you are the
Name of a shrine that does not accept double meaning as prayer or
Choleric promises or the parlance of doom declared by the waters.
The suspicious believers are buried in Jerusalem with the dolls of heaven.
My qualified eccentricities in this city are the streets with your name,
The shops that display your figure,
The lights at night that shine your face and your mouth on the breath of
Flowers from the West wind,
Infatuated with the acts of life, the tender shards of a dream.

10.28.02

Sorrow Is Not Shy

I own them, Basilicas, white bearded dictionaries that horde words made
Of gold and silver letters, great paintings of bucolic countryside that
Reflect a past epoch of peace. We are tethered to this ancient vision for
The rest of our squalid days of imitations and inbreeding consonants and

Commas. We stand when the undrinkable hearts are mentioned:
There is only one way of breathing into someone's heart that few people
Accept because flesh is the exoskeleton of intimacy. We were never
Prepared for the silence so suddenly. We are lost as public students;

We are monsters with one eye, shaped like illuminated Chaucerian
Dictionaries. We shall always be our own crisscrossing words on blank
Musical pages at the endless antipasto party in our honor. We are the
Deed they composed daily for our uncomfortable stillness when they

Talked of books among us, of the capture of the laughing death. They left
Us time to misapprehend ourselves, time to become our own artifacts, to
Camouflage what little talent we have. Bread will be eaten, water will
Turn blue and fish will laugh at our remains. This too had a beginning

Like a child has a dad at the end of each day.
Long live their hearts in their destroyed bodies, long live the poems and
Not the interpretations, long live the sexuality that blows apart the
Conservative artless language we thought was the utterances of poetry.

11.15.01

Selected Things

What is there to do until the blood dries?
We shall collect faces before the world comes to its end to meet us,
Before the fig trees bloom in Greece. We will always have time to
Demystify these events before the meaning of our lives is stretched too

Far. Meanwhile, it would be best not to die, not to rest,
Or take things too lightly, just rest and write quietly behind the door
Marked private, in the chateau where our double waits with a
Prostitute whose blue flesh sobs when touched without pay for the

Ancient services that close valves and open glands and secret contracts
Expand restoring velvet dreams of youth puzzling death on its nightly
Walks looking for Eve who lost Adam crashed into her will and lost his
Soul in the twilight of her haunches where our paths would cross:

What intimacy could death share with us at this moment of sun and
Moon? Who would drive our essential fluids to their erotic ends in their
Recombinant breaths of multiplication?
Why is it you? Is there a safe-house at the epoch where we met or

Something much simpler like our emotions?
Is this an ancestral admission or one of nature's level-headed
Commitments to us? Because we are so small,
Sometimes no bigger than a kiss when the sky is dark?

I have no place to go to except to the stone you occupy on the lake
Where all the male frogs come to be loved
And transformed to kings. Besides, dust will play its symphony for us
Regardless of the weather or the temperature of your self-esteem.

My rights are my wish to dream of folly and their construct of you
Counting how many minutes have been allotted to pleasure and despair.
Thus we are made of each other, on this narrow bridge, and time is a
Small room furnished with inexpensive truths we sometimes overlook.

11.18.02

A Case of Overwhelming Evidence

I have not thought of the value of time as we know it or how my sarcastic
Withdrawal will affect the cereal of my entropic day to day actions
And the chemical bonds between these systems we call ourselves.
Why would you interest me with the dogma of fictive fancies and illness?

I would want to prove you wrong, now that you have become the sinner's
Paint and the baksheesh of a glacier in your hand.
I am not the innocent poet that is inspired by faults and someone's
Shortcomings, nevertheless, yours are mine to cherish.

Truths are as real as lingering smells or the relocation a lonely star.
Why must I stare at my face in the morning when I shave? When your
Face is more inclusive and habitable than mine? It would be tragic to
Think the supernova of faults you mention will not become the young

Stars of my universe. I would rejoice in common passion if you thought
Of the grey lines in my head as less advanced than yours. You are surely
A lot wiser than I am: Modern physics will attest to that as my mind has
Chosen, it seems, to see you as you are and not in that cancerous village

You occupy on that childhood swing. My spirit is willing to represent its
Life with yours, if you will permit the grass to grow and the universe to
Fumble its ways through things it does not understand. Snow will be blue
In our lives as if we were the blatherskites of circumstances and entropy.

Perhaps they too will speak to us of folly and pomp, of vacations in the
Tropics, of operas my son will write of my love for you.
Why is it you explain yourself to me as an illeist would gently to a child
That this day will be his last with his dour agelasts who are his parents

Who brought him forth from gentle passions and libidinous motives that
Could not account for themselves issuing you as an automatic diversion of
Passion, one more strong affirmation that we too can survive the demons
Of intimacy in this great lake where all our rivers meet?

11.23.02

Notes from the Hazards of Life

A heart not lived in without windows or a sunny room without things to
Do at night, is a nonentity when the great winter comes to make us smell
Like humans again in this Roman attic. Up there on the small stone
Where devotion is the function of the dead, where the spider has no

Choice but to learn from the hazards of life the carelessness of children in
Their plenumad sex that is a dream shaped like the links of a chain,
Where all the arts accrete our final endings as time sleeps in cheap hotels.
Keep us in your wake and spoon feed us without

Orthodoxy to keep the plumbing free and clean of malice.
Come to bed, I have a stomachache, said the penguin to the white bear
With the a of endless bereavements in his shopping cart.
There is no thinking without daily living especially between the dark

Stitches of sleeping alone with remorse. But something always cares for
You in the dark, something that has no choice, something that does not
Care what you think or look like in the nude. Remember it is not God,
Your despair has no value to Him, only the coffee and rolls you bring in

The morning when you get to heaven on time with your menu of deeds
And photographs of your lovers who preceded you here.
It is my obligation to tell you these things before your solo is finished.
You must not arrive with empty pockets on this your last holiday with us.

Rain will wash the chemistry away and you will be left with a scrubbed
Face and no memories of the life you left behind for others to talk about
Your sanguinary choices in solitude. Anyway, when you get there,
You'll realize that your conscientious process has gotten you where you

Are, alone on a grand scale. Think of me as a pilgrim's brunch on a bad
Day in your quest for independent eternity that you think will put things
Right during the long march through the wilderness. I will march with
You and keep your pillow dry and the coffee warm and bright.

11.28.02

For a Ceremony

Our tickets are marked sorrow.
We are traveling into the final act of the great poets' lives;
They are buried on this island of drums and streamers.
The music never stops playing here,

Poets keep arriving,
Some in a hurry, still drunk on their own work.
Yet others are crestfallen for not making enough time to write,
For never having the courage to submit anything to the myths of

Publishing. Everything interfered with their notions of being a poet,
So they never were. It is Sunday morning and noon will be here with its
Tea of Chinese references to an idea, to the butterfly who became a poet
After a sorrowful spring or the beetles who become a philosopher at

Harvard where ideas are made of parchment paper.
Will it always be this way when the birds leave for warmer climes?
Why does a question have to be followed by another question to sound
Like a question? Is this some religious idea of thinking like the Torah?

Or how our minds work like the clatter of dishes in a busy diner?
See what I mean? It's not simple, anymore.
Remember when we got laid on weekends in the village?
Remorse was a cold beer the next morning and something clever to

Mention at the next party? Because everyone knew who you left with,
And asked the magic question, was she a great lay,
Was she like she acts? My friends seem to say from that dream,
"We did this all for your education, when you appeared on the scene,

You were so uncomfortable."
They are still thinking without breathing and are the stars on our
Foreheads, the customs of our poetry, our gross services to honor them,
With our dry ceremonies of writing, alone without them.

11.17.02

Notes from the Phantom Doctor

Why not leap, no one will blame you or investigate your happiness,
Your proficiencies as a sleeper.
Don't tire your friends with your wishes and puddles of solitude you have
Brought upon yourself because you refuse to validate that if you stand
Still long enough they will dry up and you will be on your own without
Reasons for human experimentation.

In time, waves realize they are not alone and other waves roll by as
Unwanted company in the experience of the ocean. So stop being the
Queen of pain and open the pages of the book, earn more money and
Sleep will not be late this year with all its chores and convictions so you
Won't notice life go by so harshly and all your limbs will grow to maturity
Without the help of heaven.

I am not talking about androgyny,
Nevertheless, I'm flattered you see me as a surprise brunch on a day
During the week and not on Sunday when it is appropriate,
According to your conscientious map of the world you inhabit
When you think the sun will shine only for you.

Other than that I promise you time well spent without the official rumors
Of final auditions. So stay away from your own body and don't pay the
Bills to keep it in good working order and leave its gentle conservation to
Me.

11.30.02

The Thorns

I am glad to get back to you. It has been too long in the making
And the rains are coming to wash away what we deserve in the way of
Happiness, which is too abstract to my recent way of life that once lacked
The thorns of intimacy:

The swat team of my confidence that moves time back
And forth like a floating target that becomes a crescendo as I think of
Gifts to me because I deserve something decent to spend time with you
On the meadows with the unicorns that adore you in the sunlight.

The awnings are annoyed at the precious fruits they cover from the
Rampaging sunlight that desires their maturity.
Resist the others, they do not understand you have to be loved for what
You think you are as this was planned for me before time could flip an

Egg, sunny-side-up, which can be quite a messy chore if you have not
Practiced for a thousand years as I have just to impress you the following
Morning so there are no disabused excuses to talk about over an
Embarrassed piece of toast who wants to drown over our conversation of

Reasons why it has been so long.
Then the pink peripheral spots come into a vision I imagined you would
Look like after tea or coffee.
Actually it was because of you that I am here so late in the evening of

Creation, not well dressed for all the nights to come.
I hope they will meet with your renaissance approval
And your immaculate eye for subtle detail?
I am very happy although your affections are in the tiniest sums,

They are so precious to me with their long operatic fingers and dark
Dresses floating between the colored columns of klieg lights.
I live for these lights and their pillars of beauty that make my sleep
Possible, and inviolate when the thorns pay their visit.

12.1.02

Invitation to a Self-Portrait

"I paint self-portraits because I am
so often alone, because I am
the person I know best."
Frida Kahlo

When my life becomes too real for my own good, I jump into the
Appetites of night, and turn the lights into a bed that reads to me of your
Life as it stands in the moonlight that provides an ambiance in my dreams
Which is the best part of sleeping. On this glacier of bitter delusion there
Is happiness without pain, there is no emptiness as all I have is miles of

Imagination where you reside with that distinguished gentleman dressed
In black, my poetry. I walk into things and lose my way in stores as tiny
As bodegas that house a forest of American beers for the natives. Herbs
And magic cards permeate my welcome when I venture into things that
Come natural to you because I lack the courage of the clouds in the sky.

But why should I get there alone? How much fun would hell be if there
Were no one in residence? And what about the vitamins of duplicity we
All take to stay ahead of things. Will my license as a poet be revoked?
What will be left of me without drinking with other poets?
These are the questions I ask myself when the sugar dissolves in my

Coffee. I take my pulse before I write and flirt with the rules of the King's
English. That's about how tough I am these days, concocting some
Excuse to run like hell from a purely hypothetical life of peace and
Reptilian spirituality. But nothing ever happens, only this preamble,
That is really scientific flagellation that induces glimmers of you.

11.21.01

Spanakopita and Taramosalata

It is the history of everything, destiny and its disagreeable compromises of
Debilitating undigested daydreams. These secretions come from the
Heart of a snowy Japanese painting that no one can afford as it is the last
One of its kind, and the artist is part of a dream that came from a
Mountain. When I smile you say I remind you of a seal, my humorous

Grin a black smudge on the white-blue ice on the other side of the world.
Not long ago truth became a ladle and is now our destiny looking for the
Consommé of desires to drown in. We have enough for every dream of
The good life to reinvent the past with words that will not violate our
Hearts in their state of recollection, constantly

Inserting meaning into abandonment violating the extremities of memory.
But Orpheus would not listen to Eurydice's supplications and laments
When she said to him "Abandon everything you think you are on earth
And come with me to be happy in hell where everything really happens
And events are a vivid recollection of the girl of your dreams."

He hesitated and the earth sealed the crevice with a shudder that would
Ring in the hearts of poets forever like a truth that occurs only once at
The end of time. Orpheus, unable to cry or utter an intelligent promise,
Turned to look at her as she slipped into the smoky train of memory.
Only life stays in love when we are gone: The flowers and the grass tear

You apart for disturbing the features of the ground because your heart is
Too big for the worms to understand the meaning of loss and the sound of
Your music does not let them sleep. It is true that Eurydice left because
The abstract actions of music drove her mad and into the dark where
There are no electric switches to begin your life over again.

4.1.02

New York Sutra

Behind me, like the shadow of the sun,
The city begins to shine on our days.
We accept the albedo of what is at hand for the one chance to live
The life that is required when we come to the surface to float

With the tones and colors of forever that the astrologers
Have assigned to us to live by in our legends that travel by day and night at
Eccentric speeds that twist time away from us.
But you know where to find me when the sky darkens:

I will be the dish of milk in the night when the shadows
When the breezes come from the other world to abate our stay
In this one, with wings and white clothing to cover this device
Of reckless organs. A vice just the same.

An evil, a piece of meat that travels from place to place that we pilot
Everywhere there is flesh stored in boxes of overrated schoolboy
Pleasures. But it is woven into the curtain of our dreams like some
Prehistoric default upon an ancient wall, like a window near the sky

Watching eclogues drift by. And from my heart your name will spring to
Name a star that will live in the back of our soul like a necklace around
The happiest islands that stood out in the distance of my life.
Do the gods really talk that way on empty street corners,

Empty of the prostitutes they admire, shining in the night like mysterious
Jewels that laugh when touched? We could pretend that nothing ever
Existed, not even your wondering question about life and the breath of an
Idea about to explode. Answer the phone, it's me,

The wrong number you dialed in a moment of romantic first names.
Weep for where you are going, expect me to be there when you arrive.
I will be the secret message you carry in your life for the lovers.
The wind will carry the rest with expression in the caricature of the future.

4.29.02

Las Mañanitas (The Little Mornings)

For "Biki"

It was Easter as I walked in the public garden of virginity, exhaling at
Every face with yours mounted on the clouds. Think of all those whose
Lives became unnecessary to themselves who are now part of a winter
Language, fading with the stars: The death by Leukemia of a grand

Master, the sparkle of poetry whose necessity ended the altered last
Page of the twentieth century. Death is an invalid and we the naive
Attendants, the employed kisses sewing the heart with emotional income.
No promised land, no hermetic sleep with any other, no fingertip secrecy,

No bombs of affection to terrorize the muse, no armpit concealment to
Give the moment something to remember like the illusive tunnels of black
Silk. We cling to these visions like small animals cling to the last morsel
Left behind by a bigger, more ferocious poet.

7.15.02

Fresh Figs

What do birds and animals have to do with gifts and mysterious talents?
You are the hero of this old story, not the trial that eventfully has
To stop and lose its way to gain identity. Yet, there are certain crises
Struggling to be what you are as you are, the magic white buffalo that
Sees and celebrates everything. It laboriously plods along without books,

Cards or lipstick, wearing tension and luck. You are confusing your
Specialty with the living. They do not matter, they are the best practical
Joke that has happened in the last 25 million years and persist on
Laughing at you and your gifts, that remind them of Hollywood movie
Gypsies. You did not fall out of a passing car by chance. I must tell you,

Repeatedly. You were born into the solitary confinement of spirits and
luck. You will pay the penalty of instant dissatisfaction, teaching you the
Agony of the outsider who never looks in, perfuming the comforts of the
Living. They left you a note that you will not read or touch because
It looks like me and reminds you of fresh figs.

6.18.01

My Life as a Book

I want to be you: Do you have one on the shelf that will fit me,
That I can wear when I think of you as a mysterious testimonial
Acknowledging my person as an event in your life? It has been a struggle
To get here, to look back to be with you. Each of my digressions has
Led to your bounteous predictions. There are not enough of you to stay

In bed for, to remember the approaching winter trapped on the wrong
Island with a letter of introduction and bouquets of mistakes to refinance
The rumors in the future. But darkness is more accurate when looking
Back at the beaches, sublime with the secrets of youth that appear
Like Roman numerals in the sand with Greek flowers in their hair.

There is enough metatherian warmth to keep us for all the winters to
Come. The strangest thing is your hair, with its many laughs and hidden
Corners of virtue that embarrassed the forms of others,
Living out their lives in the prosperation of gloom.
Only the smoke of old age will remember but never taste what we did.

7.12.02

The Shelf Life of Poetry

Time has no favorite location other than to rest in your hands depriving
The rituals of living as tears fall in all directions when the heart has no
Place to stay and the howling begins to push the snow.

The common bed of a kiss is the air where you are sleeping.
Lips part in the night like vibrating seraphs on a quest to attend an opera.
I committed the absolute crime of memory when I wandered into

Your life not wearing my characteristic chill.
My secret is safe when it listens to your delightful refrain newly released
From heaven where thorns are the hors d'oeuvre of the day,

Accompanied by a savory long list of daredevil things to do on a holiday
of awakening vulgarity and rudeness to the world.
We will repackage old and lost shortcomings, recycling the turrets,

Dungeons and masks we wore in the tower to hide the pudency of
Moonlight. Soon the whole century will come for us to envy the new
Boxes and ribbons of forfeiture that adorn each new morning.

Let us have all those things that partially shine in the light that guides
Poetry as it stumbles on its way to your heart so you will extend its
Corrosive shelf life.

9.17.03

Quietly Across the Sky on Valentine's Day

Another dream is about to expire and I will become part of its extinction
By the embellished laws you hold so dear to your courageous heart.
You manage reality in its yoke of pain so each day becomes a vacation
Brochure of gratitude. I am not supposed to be here between your toes

In your office. But I would like to begin here, proceeding to the ultimate
Destination where lips come to rest very close to sleep.
But sleep has changed the ephemeral descries and half functions that flee
Through a mélange of unrecognizable hopes. Look up to the roofless sky

Without a view of the telltale memoranda that held its place wherever
Flamboyant fluids are spilled in the dreaming rooms inheriting my
Ancestor's limitations of the color of life. Except the ones you kept for the
World to enjoy on its day off. These words cinematically inhabit the sea

Carefully and its autocratic memory. Nevertheless,
I like chocolate, Carravagio and revenge: The anonymous architect of
Jealousy that mingles illusion with bits of love.
By decree I will not be allowed to leave my memories intact,

As I am encrypted friendly fire to them because I was born in the
Renaissance, a Coptic monk with no assistance of his own except
Watching women beseech for cheese and green olive oil.
The whispering goddess has stopped pointing her finger at me,

But I am no longer her attainment.
Tragically, I have run away with the gender of her dream, and the tiny
Voices that compose her name on my adolescent soul, that lives with the
Woman of my dreams, calling to me quietly from across the sky.

2.4.02

On Greek Mythology circa 02.29.2000

The ants have our mannerisms and see our desperation in
Italics and footnotes. To the ant the weather has no
Courage. Courage can be sublime without a war.
We and the ants see things at the end of ecstasy.

Did you know ants are born philosophers and poets?
But most choose to be drones or rain.
Of the ants, drones are the ones allowed to fall in love.
They all marry the same person over and over again as we do.

By the way, Hellenic ants have no fear of Trojans usurping them
From summer picnics. They collect bits of bread, feta cheese
And irretrievable phrases, never meant to be read as classical
Episodes of our lives. I will share mine with you.

Teach me your madness, show me how to dance so I may
Become the king of Cyprus. I can never go back to the thought
I would last forever. No one lives there anymore. But those
Beloved secrets still haunt me when you laugh. I'll do what

Your heart suggests. It's intriguingly shaped like fate and looks like
The treasure map I lost when I realized short hair and dresses were
Different. They're the initials of the Northern Lights. The Gods would
Come closer to the Earth to spoil us with their future. *Agonia.*

Christus Apollo

(My memory of Kenneth Koch)

The clouds cry out to hear the hero of an accelerated life
That will not stay buried. These memories are many,
Flowers and fire wearing the faces of childlike logic.
The spirit of the best human effort once walked among us,

Who is now the stops of a majestic organ that plays his professional
Goodbyes taking his leave of us: These are the rocks of Parnassus
And the echoes of the future. He carried them a long way over the Alps,
He gave them to us at his expense to walk in our sleep with long

Dreads of poetry to make us men.
Night fell upon the eyes of the dead so we could face the gods
Without the imitators in the capital of daydreams.
He was driven by the sweet breath of deer in flight when he

Wrote the encyclopedia of torn pages and erudite verbs.
Sensing loss in a series of menologies to honor him, the lights will go out
For many of us who never knew his precious teachings of a gracious
Song. Although a few of us remain awake to sit in secret with our books

Among the poets whatever their antiquity.
O ancients, we commend to you this poet,
This wit,
With his valleys and pages of dignity,

With fierce contempt for glossal mediocrity where he remained an orphan
Like a newly cut jewel among cinders,
With his afternoon joys,
With his childish power of the air,

To restore this fallen day,
To restore our dark language
With its sad white birds weeping for wilted cherries
And for the empty space that glitters in the sun.

We wonder how he looked upon the stars.
Did they see him, too? How many stars burned beyond Orion?
Did Centauri glance at him? Among the ten trillion poems written across
The universe of wine and bread, there was one miraculous poet,

Who spoke to many voices in the dark without knowing their language.
Another birth has left us with *New Addresses*,
With eternal methods to continue free of poetic despair far beyond
Andromeda. He wrote upon the molecules of seas.

How can we make you stay? How for one breath longer?
Let us name a day, a street or a month after Kenneth,
Although it should be an epoch for every day we die with you
And go as far as possible putting our best words forward.

8.22.02

Crossing the Himalayas

My incurable decree is to go on seeking the god of dreams who cannot
Sketch the life of fire or keep little secrets or evasive kisses.
There is an army that fights for pain in the grand manner that walks upon

The earth with sad footsteps. But all the voices are right, your kindest
Kisses belong to my established envies and the older wishes redress
What comfort there is in your voice, the addiction of silence.

Dear, I know nothing of this life, but death is always near with its faultless
Murmurs, pretending to us it is our final pleasure gesticulating like a
Cloudless night in an old people's home or a cleaver machine that puts us

To sleep. The stars never expected us to stay longer than we had to and
Will not judge us if we cross the line to stay longer.
They notice the pranks, the gods being led away to join the sighs of

Lovers who do not sleep without their moments of winter nights when the
Classifications are at their narrowest point of dividing warmth from cold
Creating the star-shaped universe for the morning to come calling.

We have been led to the point of no return. It happened eons ago when
There was only honey in the innocent heavens.
Now the sky is all around us waiting for us to sleep so the bees can

Return. Tears are no longer dying for us or for despair.
They no longer have to pass by to let us know who we are,
That is what art is for, my love. The screams do not need us anymore,

We have mortified them enough with our speechless indulgences.
Those faces are washing away and have even taken their make-up off for
Someone else with less merit. The familiar quotations of eternity are no

Longer medium rare and the train is finally turning away from us,
We have been left on the platform in front of the midnight snow that used
To frighten us with our own footprints.

10.28.02

Half Life in a Myth

If there were a hero that looked at me,
I would want to be the Hellenic sea,
To say it freely with a young poet's voice,
Or in my father's native speech,

I would be a hero that would come from the arms of the sea.
I would be touched with action and as a hero of essential order,
I would teach the beauty of the eyes of the desert that are burned in my
Soul, out of nights and dreams,

I would come forth like a telescope who has seen a star for the first time
At dusk, saying to you this is the education of a short life in the heavens
That took shape in an earthly myth.
But when you say their names over and over again in the cave,

It is we who become the disciples of fire quivering at the foot of an
Image as though a man might be the image of a god or a woman taking
The form of happiness. I want to go to that country of mysterious
Dueling, and inquire after the house of Cupid where as though a boy

Might be a man and a marvel in our sleep. But I am a picture vender,
Perhaps from old Athens, who wants to stand in the doorway displaying
Images of sandy beaches and continents of language that sing as far as
The heart reaches according to the customs of art.

8.13.02

Soliloquies to an Ode

For "Biki"

This is a tale of an induced cecity, the deception of passion's evil,
Of a heart that could only face you with a pair of lips attached to its shirt,
Although virtuous and attired in contemporary intentions that always
Dwindled in cheap hotels of fading expectations.
Among these industrial and social geologies of fetal entertainment

And escapism, one would think the beating would stop and that the CAT
Scans would regress into their total sonic memories of other failing
And melting organs as life passes them by in favor of Queens and
Brooklyn where rents are not as expensive and Chinese food floods the
Streets with poets and struggling artists. I lead an impersonal life here as

Everyone works twenty-four hours a day pursuing the Asian version of the
Korean dream of prosperity in the capital of Peking Duck and General Tso's
Spicy chicken. Then I realized I was sleeping between hot tectonic plates,
That I always wanted in the community parochial therapy, that attempts
Excavating the captions of life, sex and the murder of passive parents at

The subliminal level of juvenile events of stuffed toys that pray for dry,
Sunny weather as they will become bloated when it rains on them
And their personalities will wash away like the monsoon of youth when
Any minor event could invade and wound them with the pseudonyms of

Sin and pleasure, like the kamasutra in its diaphanous Iraqi night shirt or
A bed made from the bogus dreams of the undecipherable eroticism of
Middle East. The weather in our cranial cavities has become warmer with
Understanding that our needs are amends addressed to the gods of
Honey and dates, and the bacterial ferocity of repentance as addictive as

Innocence. Will I die a farmer planting your favorite corn for the
bumper crops of mammalian festivities you invented for my prophetic
Mayan Labors? These devices of excruciating divinations are covered with
Enow for your convenience. Your outline burns the epidemic and cosmic
Events that bounce in and out of my chamberless life

Of cloudy rooms of seemingly senseless euphonies. This is no fault of
Mine since I am trapped in an energized muscle who wrestles me into an
Envelope of pulsations and beauty to the unison of prehistoric voices
(that I thought someday would be mine to keep) when humans became
Massive, ill-fed inconveniences walking the earth without shoes or lust.

1.5.02

The Way of the Samurai

What, actually, are we? Chances are we will not be holding hands when it
Is revealed to us, especially if we are screwing.
When the results become known and the rabbit has died for fear of
Becoming the parent of a human being.
How many more preordained screws to go before we get to the bottom
Of this obsession of replication?
You were always in full bloom when I drained you of that sticky stuff that
Movies and novels are made of, normal and healthy fluids on their way to
Meet the hierarchy, a living normal,
A standard organism, having fun.
But we were far too clever at simple joys,
Talking about them in mysterious terms reminiscent of witchcraft. Might
As well been at IHOP for the remainder of the experience to come as in
Returning from somewhere.
Sex should always remain like a small flower in the woods with its pale
Attraction in moonlight. Why? Because the conclusions are always on the
Same page earmarked for disillusionment. Besides,
When the results are in, we do not want to compromise destiny.
We were meant for each other,
Anyhow. Why not just bloom for each other without the epistemology
About what a great lay you are. Instead, we should think about our
Positions and how they see their way around in bed,
They thrive on noise,
You know, and mutual wresting.
It is their universe, they are staying,
We are not.

8.10.02

From the Memoirs of Count Bechamel to His Beloved

Would you have picked me as a young man to watch you undress?
Your undressing is another part of the day most of us know nothing of.
What will I do when it rains, and you are not here to cover me with your
Simplicity of logic?

How I love the weather when you are here!
As your unexpected hero, I insist on bad weather to stay alive and well.
When I tell this story, storms break and kisses lose their original
Innocence. Yet I still respond to them, despite my failures, as a human
Being, and my 20 thousand memories of them.

Why has love's frenzy chosen the heart as an enemy? It has a
Habit of never winning, except to remember its pompous loss of blood.
If you attempt to spot the flow of blood loss, it stops beating itself and
Dies. The only organ that does not want to live without wounds and a
Conscious. Its laborious specialty is to consider love a deadly antagonist.

The results are breaking the metallic rules of happiness that were
Put together by a typhoon in some former oblivion. Let us talk a long
Time, for as long as the arctic night takes to reveal our fates to the cold.

When I think of my predecessors, I cannot stay awake, they are an
Endless celebration of what love should be, although they were all
Burned by it. I suppose they, too, did not have the same advantages
Bequeathed by soporific parents: A statement to the mistress reaming my
Sough humanity.

I have spent years and money seeking a practical joke that would
End all this, but there is no profitable end in sight.

6.17.01

At the Bidding of the Muse

I marvel at your caravansary solitude and the Roman baths that greet you
On your way to meet the tribe and the others who bathe among us with their
Pugnacious egos. Retreat from shame and cultivate silly things to do, not
Alone but in harmony with the dailies of our midnight bodies.

It is not a holy city but rather an undiscovered treasure with illusionary
Military encampments full of wishes and old centuries.
Why are the ghosts so uneasy when we expose the back of our souls to
Them? Of the professed, overrated deadly seven,

Let us add solitude and despair as a verb for being dead.
We shall call it the detestable eighth that chose not to kiss the dark with
Its thin lips. But I have sworn by the eyes of the city that my papers are
In order to enjoy a weekend of personal use.

These patterns of speech are not liberal or polite as we are subject to
This nomenclature that creates vulnerable sounds.
Unlike our stomachs, the ear does not enjoy chewing and can subsist on
Air and murmurs and cries in the night where God's heart is a fine

Omelet to be eaten with life and bread at Christmas dinner to celebrate
The gluttony and mystery of the holy murder when the sun went down,
The retainers whose creed is the eatable calories of sin so we are finally
Gourmets of the feathers of beauty.

The first bite is a smile or a casual meeting that does not pray to a
Bleeding heart that has since scattered over the earth like green paint.
I have sworn by the night to become your weekends and my personal life
Will be a shrine to the dragon of romance who craves our aspirations in

The circle of life. It is all music and gossip, if not painful, but amusing to
Hear the cognates and lovers of absence on the anvil shaped like a heart
In this politely ruminating dream of proposals and flosculent proclamations
Seated at the head of the table when we arrive as one-sided

Travelers with expectations seldom repeatable. In most cases,
Fantasias are romantic routines of passion on the fork of attention that
Do not remember the act of fucking their way through the empty
Dormitories of fixations, since our infantile appearance at the bidding of
The muse.

12.4.02

Bright Blue Self-Portrait

I thank the spiders' webs and the circus dancers who stain our eyes with
Rapid movements and authorize our handcuffs to make no distinction
Between night and day or love and hate.
No one will know the sum of our arduous daily separations from bed to

Work. These pillars actually belong to you since I have not counted them
Or know any more than you do where they are or in what country they
Still exist. We can put all our concerns into a loaf of bread and French
Kisses, go to movies and watch the splashing milk on the screen imitate

The forest in the moonlight. Why all the fuss about the patrons becoming
Feathers, discharging their ideas of nobility on the evening news? There
Are no lights in the theater just soft snow from the balcony that is the
Little red schoolhouse where all this began.

Actually it was because of you I did not attend as often as I should have.
I was too embarrassed to face you across the clay modeling tables since I
Always felt like the clay in your hands was a cartoon version of my teen
Years, dear slippery-fish ladies of the sleepy west.

Don't forget, my early life will be yours, too,
With its self-descriptions of poetic justice,
The tiny creatures we write about can describe themselves in the moss
We leave behind.

12.5.02

The Black Song of the Apple

This body of errant deeds, of fake routines in the wilderness,
Between the realms of assurance,
Of Adam and Eve's bedridden romance,
Since the inception of my initial forty thousand sighs,

And the blended colloquian of my flesh with its antipathy to the world of
Infantile celibacy,
Is why I don't read in bed.
Don't you know it is the battlefield for the already mortal representatives

And slaves of human salt that we often pay the highest price to,
To retain the right to inhuman happiness,
The day-wasters who wear their damage as the blemished emblems of
Some forgotten occult gospel threatening to disband the word of the

Loving for the world of the recalcitrant makers of hell who declared me
Missing to the deaf, in the country of confession, each day is a private
Cavity, when bowing to the barefooted contraption we call romance.
Forbidding the world a dress code and the meaning of sexually unwanted

Hairs and their neurotic scent of adventure in the glossolalia of the abyss,
The hole in the ozone is where we wind up like collapsed sacks of pills
With bright waxy mortuary smiles and as bloated as socked figs,
Threatening the endangered naturally dead.

When I was a fetus I had a whipped tail and was in love with a large
Mammogram that had a siamese twin sister that said I was a precious
Bird born to an ancient aqueduct. The reason is I wanted to be her
Secret saddle and harvest her words from the twilight when she would

Char my soul for wanting to stop wanting the meat of shame.
I wanted to redo the black song of the apple I would have given her each
Day as an offer I would not be ashamed of. I would have deleted my
Body and emailed the rest to her as a token of destiny.

12.6.02

Pages of Night and Day

The sacred spells are equipped with the latest animivorous machines to
Ameliorate the endings of all capital letters in folk tales that have kept us
Apart with the childlike odorless substances whose value is the

Competitive tautological events of sadness.
Like most things passed on to us by the purveyors of echoes,
We have been herded together to witness our first distressed adoration.

But you were built to last without leaks and amblyopic quarter tones.
Uncannily I am still here with what is left of my life among the inhuman
Remains of art, with their herbs of egotism that offer gangrel purpose to

Survive the enantiomorphs' particles of fame,
Attached to an old house of measured proverbs that blow in on doses of
Wind. The perfect kiss, of its own volitional happiness performs and

Creates the tissue of the soul and the stamina of the flesh becomes a
Secondary patch of light held together with escape routes when the hours
Of joy are counted for the last time and given to the gods of silent

Actions. We are deadly subscribers of gossip and to the cowbells of the
Past. So let me be the unidentified kindness and the motherless profile of
Time while we last and before the empty room is taken captive by the law

Of bodies passing their due to the night. The day joys of thought, more
Private than daydreams and their vast acquaintance of what we stand for
To our family photographs that discourage growing up to meet

Their vocal expectations at the end of public life.
The dead, once our friends and high mentors, are the enemies of common
Speech as we knew it before their leave.

Since then, they are the sacks of comic silence with mixed feelings toward
Us, the sadly living unable to speak to them as we fumble through our
Endless unfinished business. Are they wearing cosmic medals for us,

Left behind for us to wear to defend them and their public accusers of
The written word with all their sententious old baggage and camouflaging
Modern Latin syntax? So we honor the recently and not so recently dead

By pulling new faces out of the hat we cannot wear to match our ties
Of consciousness that comes through with the stench of the past to
Intoxicate the symptoms of our neglected craft.

But they are welcomed to our untidy poems loquacious with wordy
Circumstance. Their works are proof they ended our makers with whom
We colluded as the wired sixties took us hostage with whiskey,

New ideas and eulogies for some brilliant literature at the tavern where
We buried faith each night for those yet to be dead.

12.12.02

Withered Invitations

For on this Christmas the adornment is the word and the outer limits of
Abusive embraces that plead ignorance when you come in the room
Flowing with tears. The aftershocks of intimacy suffer humiliating
Distress with your favorite issues, such as "we are alive and deserve to

Die, too. They are dead, therefore, abandoning us, they deserve to die,
Too." It does not feel warm anymore when the golden ribbons of
Summer finally arrive as you are probably aware we are without them.
But we have their wounded pages and some a scribbled note not

Effortlessly deciphered, yet, a note from one Master.
There is nothing we can do, the stage manager will be furious for
Interfacing the ambitions of the living with the snowballs from the
Sickness of heaven. No one foresaw this deadline. Art is always spring

And warm blue skies to the Gnostic beholder. I won't explain why I live in
The doorway on the marble steps in front of the white door. It reminds
Me of the ambitions of desire, the blue lights of lust and the white lights
Of oblivion tie themselves together to survive to be with you and falling

Out of a glabrous life for happiness to be with you. I am the oldest lie in
Captivity, the oldest lost man looking to lick your lost minutes away at
Midnight. I can shrink, too, and live inside of you without ever disturbing
Your definition of being violated.

12.15.02

Swaying the Allure of Dreaming

Let's stay by the seashore and say little; we can say it's worth the silence,
At least the pit that divides our hands is worth the avowal:
They won't open to each other in vain.
I commit mine to yours and my actions when I flow in yours.

I know mine are not the strongest
And lack purpose without the warmth of life.
But I believe, nevertheless, if you hold nature to its simplicity in these
Matters, you will become more mysterious and your writing will illuminate

The unsolved hearts you often write about.
Do not ask for the answers now which cannot be given you because you
Could not live them. Perhaps you indeed carry them in your laptop but
Have not taken the time to flush out the screen of its fits of

Depression because you move from place to place to write your memories
Of things that are to be, that I have done so often to no avail.
So let's live the question now. With it will come complete trust and
Ablution from your most intimidating desires,

In the shade, under the spell of the forest
Take what comes, if only from your will to go on:
Sex is boundless and difficult; yes.
But it is the difficult that will join us, almost everything is difficult,

And everything is serious and difficult,
And everything is serious. We both chose this café to be anonymous to
Embarrassment. But we take our experiences as our best passions,
Especially the ones floating in the nearby past with their childhood

Strengths to achieve an entirely new life,
Not influenced by convention or custom, you need no longer fear to lose
Yourself and become unworthy to your most savage obsessions.
Your body will become pure seeing and my hand won't matter in yours.

Questions and Answers

My angel, don't think the great stillness is wooing us:
We just haven't slept the same among the letters that have a habit of
Recognizing us. Those beautiful letters live in Paris all year around.
For even the best of men go astray with words within the gentle depths

When they are to express something unutterable.
But I believe nevertheless that you need not be left without them as a
Part of me, as a recreation between hesitations,
The boundless ones in moments of doubts.

If you have this affection for things that don't really matter to the poor,
Then everything will become clear, more coherent and somehow more
Conciliatory, not perhaps how I manage to function from day to day
Taking Kenneth's last words to be my daily gospel that "we must write

Every day," but in your innermost consciousness and wakefulness you will
Know I have patience with these black lines that I share with my most
Intimate friends to say I'm still writing to you.
So I sincerely beg you to have no remorse with matters of the heart,

For it is a foolish, overbearing organ that does not have a place to rest
Except in our sleep with dreams it cannot have during our times of
Playful awareness. I only seek, as well as I can, to serve the last
Wishes as a poet. What else is one to do with these unsolved hearts on

Paper? Otherwise they are of no use to anyone but the dreamer who tries
To cherish matters of the heart, like closed rooms to the public in some
Grand museum filled with treasure, or like books written in a strange
Tongue hidden in the library of moments we let slip away fearing it was

What we wanted from the beginning. We stopped searching for the Answers because we could not live in their blue tents. It's a matter of Living everything. Live now, and perhaps you will then gradually, without Noticing it, one distant day live right into the answers of the heart.

8.3.03

Appendix

Frank Lima: The Poetry of Everyday Life and the Tradition of American Darkness

by David Shapiro

To Elaine de Kooning

Frank Lima's poetry is a poetry of everyday life, but only a poet of enormous strength and fearlessness is capable of describing the everyday. One might say that the life Lima describes is so exceptional that it cannot or should not be placed under the idea of the everyday. But I think his inventory of traumata in childhood, of drugs and dangers, of incarceration and release, of his triumphs as a man, a father and husband, a cook, a translator, an artist—this inventory in its inclusiveness of urban space is exactly what the French thinker Lefebre meant by the production of the everyday. Lefebre suggested that the real philosophy of modern life could be accomplished by the description of a single day. Lima, learning from poets as various as Villon, Neruda, O'Hara, Lowell, and Corbière, emerges with a mixture of day and dream that is a maximal realism and rendering of his more than half-century of living. It's a story of survival and, crowned by his compassion, much more than any facile listing of a victim's horrors. He concludes this volume with extraordinary poems of religious depth and poems that create a public, even vatic voice—poems for all victims, for a Hasidic youth, for those bombed in Oklahoma, for an older mortal prophet, and for his own children glimpsed in their fragility and resilience.

This development towards poems of wisdom is an unexpected delight and a sign of his status as a major poet. When I met him in 1962 Frank Lima had already written extraordinarily sensuous descriptions of the street and the body, and he had already conquered any timidity in poems that shocked everyone concerning incest, drugs, and violence. Instead of pursuing this as a single reductive mode, Lima accepted influences and worlds that made him larger and richer. He showed a disdain, he once told me, for Beat poets who wanted to return to a poverty he wanted to transcend. He was always willing to look backwards and even with nostalgia he studied, but he had a ferocious way of engulfing new experiences. After the first volume, and early poems that are as poignantly particular and sharp as prison slang, he learned from Frank O'Hara and wrote poems that sweep us into abstractions and stories that are mythical and urbane and humorous. He had always had this humor, as in his eerie comparison of a lover to a judge of the criminal courts, but the poems now accepted and assimilated a disjunctive poetics of the New York School. He loved this tough art of welding disparate poetic worlds, and dedicated his own art to that of David Smith's heraldic and monumental sculpture.

He has never stopped learning, never stopped being a student of himself, language, and the city. He became a master chef, cooking having always been one of his talents, received a master's degree from Columbia with the same earnestness that had led him to study Villon in his teen years even while in rehabilitation, and he has now become the master of a magical-realist style that I identify with Marquez as much as Neruda. Strangely, he has turned a prose fragment into a dazzling lyrical-narrative autobiographical sequence. In the future, we may expect more from this novelistic mode that includes amazing cinematic sequences, for example, a horrifying scene in which he observes his father drunk and near death in a park. Lima, a New York Surrealist, completely seizes the rage and detachment and strangeness of this vision. It is something he accomplishes from his earliest work, but now it is not just snapshot photography at its best—no small achievement itself—but a masque-like architecture of great scale, where the instants add up to a whole social vision.

After our first amazing meeting, I was touched by what Kenneth Koch called, in his introduction to the first chapbook of his poems, his courage and his honesty about pleasure and poverty. These early poems are still luminous achievements, and there can be no anthology of the last fifty years of poetry that does not include something of these amazing poems without a loss. No poem that I know of speaks like "Mom I'm All Screwed Up" about childhood torments and its ferocious intimacies. No city poems about Spanish Harlem have ever yielded the completely convincing tones of these early works. They are fast, furious, and alive with the musical grace found in this sudden bit of landscape and church music from "Abuela's Wake":

> *Dios te salve Maria*
> *Dios te salve Maria*

    outside
        the snow-mouth of December tinked on the windows

"Pudgy" rises to the sweetest and most serious sensuality in "O my chocolate princess I / lay in bed / smelling of Lifebuoy soap and toothpaste / light a stogie and watch the smoke / unshoe ghost-nude thoughts." This is a poetry of a young man with great insight into the body's possibilities, but it is important to realize that he didn't stop with this kind of expressiveness.

He went to school with the "ordinariness" of the New York School and the empiricism of his great friend and mentor, Frank O'Hara, and always learned too from the perfected finesse of

Kenneth Koch. With such a different vision, it is hard to believe that he could synthesize these elements, to subulate them into his turbulent scenes: "where the fish bring light to the sun / waiting for the weakness of a dreamer." But that is exactly the task of his middle-period lyrics and prose in which he mixes hedonism, picturesque whimsy, and his particular form of honesty, emerging with extraordinary strange tales of the ordinary as in his "½ Sonnet," or his suddenly violent "Plena" or "Postcard" or "Patchouli." If his usual forte and dramatic instrument was naturalist description, he had now expanded his palette to include something as large and "anthropologically" vast as his "Cuauhtemoc": "I always bring captives here I and let the grapevine choke them."

The snapshot aesthetic of Robert Frank is thus given a funny and more intense inflection when it collides with the possibilities of a kind of historical or historicized surrealism. The search for the marvelous should not be mere and should not cut poetry off from its worldliness: "The face of poetry is an expressive cut of meat that gives us a glimpse of truth." Lima has a tremendous, almost compulsive need for truth-telling, and one remembers that Paul Goodman once suggested that poets did not write novels, not because of a lack of imagination, but because they had a compulsion to avoid fiction in a love of wild truth. This is why Lima's New York School use of symbolism and surrealism never led him away from his solid sense of thing and fact, boundless body and outside private street. If anything, he reminds us that the Surrealists at their best—one thinks of the Aragon that Benjamin loved in *Paysan de Paris*—were a final if seemingly superstitious stroke of realism in its extremity. Lima's works, like Schwitters' Merz constructions, are towers of the convoluted debris of everyday life and not reduced ejaculations or cries of protest. This is what Koch admired early in their lack of moralism, and it is to his credit that even in this sense, Lima has been able to develop, so that strangely his new moral-religious odes are willing to add to his snapshots of the marvelous in the everyday a new cognitive dimension. His integrity in developing this moral dimension might be said to occur in poems in which he is more parent than son, more citizen than nomad.

Thus, I find Lima's journey from the poems of prison, drug-addiction, and the frenzy of sexuality to his new poems and autobiographical narratives to be a triumph of what Erik Ericson used to speak of as the antinomy of wisdom and bitterness. In these poems, again and again, his early toughness is matched by a gentle largeness of generosity and something elegiac that seems necessary and not politically pretentious. He can write about the "shadow of the twentieth century" because he feels it, in Keatsian negative capability, "on my liver," and thus his ode to the Cedar Bar poets is as personal as the most personist of O'Hara. I think any critic will want to praise the imaginative vividness, syncretism, and "publicness" of these new orchestral poems. It is enough to tell the truth, though O'Hara used to joke that that was all that was necessary and form was as simple as a good fit in clothes, but the truth slant as in Dickinson is the proper opaque for a master like Lima of what I have called the tradition of American darkness.

I have always admired Lima's Whitmanesque wit and wisdom, and I recall that he once laughed back at an older poet who had told students at Columbia that they needed more solitude, "I've been in solitary and I don't need more solitude." I like his human and humorous poems, and in his late poems, like "Father's Day," he creates his own apotheosis and dissemination: "I have seen the seeds in our seeds / Become an army of paper children . . . An imperfect father gives his / Children a drawing of an old Sun." He can be as gently attenuated as a Valery Larbaud in his food poems ("Ode to Julia Child"), but these are just his most recent scherzi. The new magnitude in his work is seen in his homage to an ancient Mexico and to the tenderness of poets: "Allen will be taken from us / to the slaughterhouse of dear God." Somehow I trust his Jewish and his Catholic poems, his poems of an unbearable ethnicity, and his poems of a soaring universalism. Isaiah Berlin has taught us to dream less and less of an homogenized world of unconflicted happiness. Lima is a tragic pluralist, who knows what it's like to be almost run over in social collisions. He has gone from a poem as subtle and slangy as "In Memory of Eugene Perez" to a poem as sustained and furious as his "Oklahoma America." I have always enjoyed the way Frank Lima disdained poets who too greedily used their origins to gain a false publicity. He has an amazing lack of self-pity, both in his poems and in his presentation of himself, but I do pity those who neglect his voice and wise rage at their peril. I think Lima's story and his fabulous dark insistence are one of the most remarkable American triumphs. We have witnessed, in these thirty-five years, along with his friend, that amazing cubo-futurist Joe Ceravolo, the creation of a mature American poetry of everyday darkness.

Frank Lima could have stopped when he had finished his Rimbaldian poems of the street, rough and physical and full of caricature. He could have also accepted complacently his re-formulation of the New York School and stopped as a poet with a control of surrealism and urbane fancy. He has refused to stop, and his poetry today has the rare public-private synthesis that counts, and a supernatural naturalism that underlines him, in M.H. Abrams's sense, as a late Romantic. He finds in the turbulent darkness of New York and America his mythology, his Alps, his truth.

New York City, 1996

Index of Titles